out of everywhere 2

out of

**linguistically innovative poetry
by women in north america & the UK**

everywhere 2

edited & introduced by emily critchley

REALITY STREET

Published by
REALITY STREET
63 All Saints Street, Hastings, East Sussex TN34 3BN, UK
www.realitystreet.co.uk

First edition 2015

Cover images by Sara Wintz

Typesetting & design by Ken Edwards

A catalogue record for this book is available from the British Library

ISBN: 978-1-874400-68-4

With thanks to the publisher, Ken Edwards; partner in proof-reading, Ann M Hale; partner in life, Seaton Gordon; and all the poets!

Not all poems are complete or continuous from within the original collections, but, with the writers' permission, some text has been elided, some starts *in media res...*

Emily Critchley

'Now: to let go what we knew
to not be tight, but
toney; to find a world, a word
we didn't know'
    Eleni Sikelianos, *The California Poem*

For my daughter, Elena

Contents

To the Reader

"out of everywhere," says factual self
but are there precursors to being beside self before birth of it.
Sara Wintz,
Walking Across a Field We Are Focused on at This Time Now

It is twenty years since Ken Edwards and Wendy Mulford of Reality Street invited Maggie O'Sullivan to edit an anthology of contemporary linguistically innovative poetry by women in the US, Canada and the UK – the first of its kind to be published in Britain. Happily, today more formally original, politically and philosophically engaged poetry is being written by greater numbers of women than ever before. Here, then, is the chance to encounter some of it, in the sequel to that groundbreaking book: *Out of Everywhere 2*.

But is there *still* a need for an all-female anthology of avant garde poetry today, I hear some of you ask? My answer is in the years of careful labour that have gone into making this book, and the decision to keep its original title too. Certainly, there is no lack of prominent female writers in mainstream British poetry worlds – represented by national newspapers, poetry journals, prizes, and school curricula – a world which still holds sway over "poetry's cultural capital" in this country.[1] In the UK, we even have a female laureate for the first time. Yet, as events in the "alt lit" scenes both here and in North America continue to prove, misogyny still lurks not far beneath the surface of what are meant to be some of our most advanced experimental writing and thinking communities.

Even if we bracket the politics of these writing scenes, and attendant, vital questions of publication, dissemination and promotion, O'Sullivan's claim, in her introduction to the original *Out of Everywhere*, that "much of the most significant work over recent years, particularly, in the US [...] is being made by women" holds truer than ever and would in itself justify the existence of this anthology. Furthermore, the much larger proportion of British poets included in the sequel (roughly half) shows something of a sea change in poetic practices this side of the Atlantic. No longer does there seem to be "a dearth of women writing experimentally in Britain", as I wrote back in 2007 in *Jacket*[2] – a transformation, or at least increased visibility of one, in a very short space of time. In large part this is due to the dedicated labour – of reading, publishing, teaching, reviewing, organising, and so on – of many of the writers in the original *OOE* and of the writers in this sequel too.

There is a contemporary wave of confidence and camaraderie, facilitated by the public-private slippages the internet allows: the speed with which writers can link up with other writers, and writing, across the world; the ability to be in or out of everywhere or anywhere at the click of a button. For instance, the formation of an all female British writers' listserv in 2012, inspired by various long-standing American models, has become a necessary hub of writing, thinking, campaigning and supporting activity.[3]

Indeed, despite an increased number of entries (44 poets) there is *too much* talent to be represented exhaustively here. I regret all omissions. I plead the usual constraints of time and space. I hope that the sheer variety of the work selected will go some way to making up for that not featured. What follows can only be a partial snapshot of a moment in literary time. Likewise it is impossible to do justice to the rich diversity of the poets included and their substantial oeuvres. Much of what follows has been lifted from longer poetic sequences, project-oriented work, and cross-genre engagements with, especially, visual, performance and sound work. I can only hope that the poetry here will, as the original anthology did, inspire readers to look further into this exciting field, to appreciate and be challenged by some of the most important writers of our time.

EMILY CRITCHLEY

January 2015

1 As noted by Carrie Etter in her excellent introduction to *Infinite Difference: Other Poetries by UK Women Poets* (Shearsman Books, 2010).

2 "Post-Marginal Positions: Women and the UK Experimental/Avant-Garde Poetry Community, A Cross-Atlantic Forum", moderated by Catherine Wagner. *Jacket*, 34 (October 2007) http://jacketmagazine.com/34/wagner-forum.shtml

3 It must be noted that this increased activity is in part a reaction to the violent, sometimes anonymous, misogyny also facilitated by the internet. As Andrea Brady, the founder of the British women's listserv, recently put it in an email to me: "we seem to be living through a new wave of feminism in response to this, and the re-articulation of a bold and assertive feminist identity both within poetry and outside it is a positive consequence of what seems in many ways a very dire and regressive surge of violence towards women especially concentrated in digital environments." (Andrea Brady, email to author, 21 November 2014.)

Sascha Akhtar

from Legatura / (Ligature)

EVOLUTION

Water, yellow-green oblong
transparent legs
running through

End in fingers, drip tap
glass thick frosted hotbox
growing, human
growing

Moth floats, still.

CITY

Skyscraper, blue
tango pass night
plumes leather
head catch elevator

Tunes, catch word
hoard blanket over
skyscraper jelly
wish eye scratch

Ball, every hair
traffic float blue
earth lounge visit
gash light calm

Speck, turning.

HIGHWAY

Silver, perch
shaman blue road
cats eye dim
breaker hush fail

Hush, calypso ray
call oxygen
sparkle ligament shoe
fill momento ears blow

Leaves, perpendicular
sun cinnabar teeth
spell turnip crack
limoge iron weather

Dust, running.

HOUSE

Dream, hats my
all possess homies
shadow place box
garden little

Magick, eggblue
umbrella paper
marbleblue
kitchen hexe

Austria, fly
broom iridescent
plasticwhite
unicorn offer earth

Hangman, hanging man.

ROCOCO

Lady, basilica
charmeuse leave
savage crimson match
torque angeletta

Salve, basta
basta aura pigeon
skim tiffany sheer
ripple nest marionetta

Fall, elf gem
cislunar chevelure
glisten cherry
boat ink

Molten, moiré.

FAINT

Sleep, restful
place recharge ssh
mind veil draw
close peace

Bed, wish
embolism woman
better girl than
re-invent

Heel, licorice
warm black blossom
orange page linger
scent page settle

Hell, decimals.

PETRARCHAN BLUES

Innamoramento, skin
brunette fair mountain
my top my top

Today, blackhair of
skinpale brilliant
less blackbrown
dressed red not

Today, flashinghair of
skintalcum mauvedeep
wears sparkle voice

Stresses, s's.

POND

Bastard by way of
continent seething
(*ghoom rahee hoo*)
spinning am I, Bulleh
drift continent

Lengthen, shadow
winter creep
sunshine my
muscle tone

Clocks, white razor
beat breast
sword with head
mourn delilah

hair, cut.

*

Grooves
burn, stupid
enzyme, click
palace

Knight squirrels
rid follow me
redder I swear
vase
than most.

POET

Watch, hard words
smack away they come
come smack, mind
deceive object subject/object

Lullaby, rush single
naked burner back
burner on the fly
verge arms

Akimbo, dagon night
virtue shiver
slower shiver slower
under belly, under

beast.

NIGHT

Ice, carved flies
drip luminous eye
compound voice
sweats letter

bulbs, hallucinate
beef lilly grass
newspaper scream
press hell

button, rock on
smoke sucker cuts
run jacked up dawn
alley bull belt

Melt, horizon.

DAY

Pseudo-groove, rabbit
recover shuffle
trouble record night
cleaver bliss hover

Hungry, flat antelope
glisten tater-tot slam
slave repose bubbles
drink air

heat, turn sky
cream lacquer hand
foot face white
nose-bleed blush

Grip, tender.

SIGHT

Go slowly, good night
1000 triggers
pulled in my
head-rudder

Anxious-points, a finger
strain memory pulls
through barbed
eye-fret

Cotton, alight taste
terror shifts pulse
clasp neck swoon
love her skull-river

Flesh, bright.

Amy De'Ath

from Lower Parallel

Lower Parallel

A teal balance and ombre heart you have. What limb thrown down-
stairs hallway when I discovered prosody like thin paint like discourse
    presumes us

What prosody like blown-up flower and dripping box, coming up on an open
state and running dog, going out on starry starry axial breaks,

clear breaks onto a ravine of translucent history, now a sensitive cult a purity lunch
in the *green zone*, never a side of me you seen, never a side of me.

Beauty had a hot and final temper. Add a bit of money and a shitty life, fear-
mongering or just hanging around in here, then lay down between a fork

and a tunic. But lay down against her, more august than the three of us
o brother irenic, into the laundry coin slot I will go with you into streaming,

angel sleeping, feather down, downloading, The Simpsons, South Park, Donald and
Daisy Duck, Family Guy, Felix the Cat, Christopher Wren, Power Outage,

Moral Outrage, Disillusionment, how pathos lies at the root of all this as
the dead roll to the foot of the bed, say "womb" is a verb, "aborted" is a feeling.

A teal balance and ombre heart you have. In the Lost Lagoon,
no more illness to speak of, not homeless in the void or walking the plank

& if the present roars I don't hear it. Woke up from dream of municipal ska-
ting and the rhetoric was meaning, the actual history of women and the body

and women as a body but a man manifested the only body the only one
Marx got, resembles me not in thought or love, but eternally working

as an orange grove does, as a child does among hypermedia, as a
person who is a hotline after feudalism, as an image sprints back to reclaim us

love will save us love will save us love will save us love will save us
as if it would be classical to be bitter and cowed, down to the duck, the swan

and the holy goose, laughing out there in crack of the coast, in the echo of
Vancouver, buoyant and stupid.

*

People were talking to themselves, then troops came along like water in a hole
And crazy, mapping out pinnacles in literary history under which you

are forced to see yourself as an episode: a yellow floating condom or worse, a
standard castle in France & more affordable than Queens, a lucky conveyor

of sentiment and eager to please, carousel of polytechnics / antiseptic tourist
   tooth-glare.
How to move in and rain on you, and move you a moment closer to

the sun, against the wall a static woman, a limited psycho. Still: lower parallel,
   lower still.
Here's a population of rage at you, there is a heaped tenderness consumed

Here is a lover made of Stalins, there is a book someone wrote in
against their desire or will, in 1871, in 1989, a common logic structurally grounded

like so much neo-colonial confetti.

And now I don't believe it, and now I believe it.

And now I don't believe it, and now I believe it.

A teal balance and ombre heart you have. Or what the remote-control star
says to the intricacy of planets and kids. Opacity begging for crystal,

find a name for her, I fear for my house and garden, find a name for me,
if you lose your boyfriend, find a name for that sedimented truth

and for the vaporized Rocky Mountains that made you compete against
your own body, as it traces nothing, find a name for another pretender you
   believe in

from Caribou

Vertigo Valley

You arrived – it was unanticipatable, some bees even sang
into a future cloud very far away and yellow.

You are never perverse. You have never been perverse. You can!
A dog takes up loving on the empty gate just as other things happen
like you fall asleep, Shakespeare dies but Noroit is resurrected.

How will I know the heat from the cold and his pirate gang?

I feel the cold. I have a statue of my self that looks atonal
speaks   'the most lovable of all'   'once the reader
learns to respond'   'abate one tot'   ... I respond too.

*

I mean I don't swap souls e.g. I don't see how accidentally
touching excuses this, I wasn't sure how to life Spring into flight
and learned to respond by
     studying seagulls hard
wanting their pecks to last through hunger *and* forever amen, ugh
all the kindness, pseudo-Buddhism I want to totalise or live in, by
the world without books, pornographic bibliographies or
Turkish cuisine I respond by saying blanks out loud
embarrassing all types of metal strip clubs as well as bedside lamps
and cats eyes honey wells, but what does the flower say?

Flower, what is it you want to do – boy oh la la, *les chapelles
de mes elles! Invincible* Flower, Let this Spring be the one, let notes be dogs,
     is the body time
the time when your assiduous eyeball meets mine and our breastplate
glows on the surface   of a retrograde moon?
O my flower O my rodeo.

Listen to my kiss, let me have this joke on you and sit on it
                                        listen to my ass
the start of a new heart which does heart your curry-stained destiny.
Does swell the lake. Does heart your ass then sit on it. Keeps me off the street,
    springs two animals at peace.

*

Now I'm real nakedness some kind of hay bale girl a goofball
actress jumping rivers in the Comic Adventures of Boots.
Coming to terms with nearly two million people revealing
London's Caribou to be not me but *you*,
still for some time I am yours, for
    some life let me make this

                    s'up to you

I can't, I'm so moved by the Pacific furniture. That we have
    never spoken that we
might meet in a poem one day maybe even this one I have
stood next to you that night, simple phrase-boy, you have sat down next to me.
You banged your head on your cat mask then came up with 100 sexy ideas.
Your kisses were even better live   snapping in the ocean
                                out of love cream floats.
What relief, to relinquish all fauna
give it up to the vague princes who used to be my enemy
but lately just bounce my stare back through the windows of hydrogen buses.
Because I have the golden ticket   plus coupons and vouchers,
what cannot be achieved I am not sure exactly   watching hot ducks quack,
            shiny compact duck bodies swept along the road.

*

It doesn't matter I'm your syndicat d'initiative, go bounce
    in the night –
hug me, I'm your girl. I will not talk tonight when you are in a spell.
When you are land and sea tending to huddle in your
treetrunk counting rivets I always find you are over 2,000 years old
and without fail I already know this but am always shocked.

What are you doing now I hope you will come back,
                    I ah   oh,
my gorgeous girl, to resume and get closer to the present

I will I ever be here
with you? Perhaps we'll die before the bats come back.

Ice Land is expansive it makes sense to make me your Miss Lonely
and I will be Lonely too I will disintegrate happy into dust &
settle on your skin and form diamonds with you. Will I ever write
a Poem will you write this with me I don't think so I can do it.
        I don't think poetry
I don't think, the difference is important on the hardly seas
not to a new ghost.
            I'd like to know I am always present I always
        sing to you
even when you're spelled
all the wild things wild leaves suddenly make me welcome.
Now I am conducive to everything.
Note today outside of notebooks in the
splayed plumage of our shared brain,
it doesn't matter even what I am doing if your head is turning
        beautifully to the left is
turning beautifully.

from Erec & Enide

Poetry for Boys

That the Joy will soon come and make you suffer!

i.
Lay low in the words of the wood,
very subtle, not immune,
lay down in the snow and incline,
you are rest enough and dowry,
in the lay and the spook of an age,
very poor, still glamour,
still further than you think even
more, from the day duly swallow,
to the real green day in the dream,
very full, cracking bough,
the undoing publicity of meaning
all the whole black sky is feeling
the screwing over, resin delight
delightful residual meaning, still night.

ii.
I'm a weeping boy and a centaur caving in.
Adventures, find me – I'm hard to come by.
In the days when mirrors were made of burnished silver
I stayed up late,
in the nearly beautiful night I stood not quite
in the shower plenty natural and the water washed into
the time of my skin. I imagined how to answer the question of whether
psychic malady is a personal affair. Then I wrung
my hair and dye came out.

If I had the money to dip in being a boy,
if I was Anna O., & fallen into autism or
steeped in prelingual glimpses of Lena's face,
I'd be living system: looped in my own elements.

A system closing talking only to itself.

vii.
Down dampen sully unknown
because you ate the sunshine,
asunder among the porch-light
a tune to know, of history's mesh
an epistolary flash of deer
young, always in fashion, in brave
pursuit, climbing down a piece
of fruit to get to the last boy in
town, who ate the town and
whipped his jacket up to the
wind and ripened on a cloud,
a compensating cloud in glut, and
he fell down, he fell upon those
vandals, he was a feat of sunshine.

viii.
Boys and solipsists are written out and I pant for boys in
appellatives, I'd eat your hair and holes my God.

I call them puissant debtors and lavish roadies
or whatever you want.

I sleep in nature where warrens
serve as nail bars

I'm a stubborn boy and poised
at that beat replaced in love.

wherever my body takes precedence
I do not owe a boy, either.

it's like this forever

...

Wherever I am, Hello boy.
I do not owe a law, either.

Mei-mei Berssenbrugge

Endocrinology

1

The bird watches a man and woman dance. He touches her stomach. There's
  circulation around her
in intercapillary space, empty or hollow, in relation to organs. A virus transfers
  firefly genes
to a tobacco plant. The plant glows in the dark. How much evolution derives
  from "something in the air,"
not a square of light about a niche in a white wall. Light, your intestines. Fluid,
  lines of light. As if,
when you think about something, it already has a frame that's *a priori*. Think
  before that moment, freedom is inside there.
Think before the man and woman, their freedom of an animal among silvery
  trees. Which trunks light hits is an endocrine
permutation, a state of being or a physical space. Hormones are molecules,
  material, invisible. Their flow is random,
mesh through which a body is sense, not an image. The form of her body is
  important,
as how she is here, though there's no physical evidence of her physical
  suffering.

2

Hormones provide a mechanism by which the body relays chemical signals
   through cells perfused by blood.
There's a structural need to make tectonic episodes which might otherwise
   become pliant.
Conceiving of the body as a space of culture tends not to refer to it as nature,
   unless it's been taken away by disease,
hairy ears, genital ambiguities, like a shamanistic object, not generic. Because
   she's in a body, it makes decisions.
Black rock in a dry river, weeds tangled at the base, something heavy enmeshes
   with something light.
The material, of non-negotiable contingency, the feeling, a different structure
   on different physical levels.
A pool in the forest gleams with organic matter, its depth of the possibility of an
   imbalance in the body,
when luminosity detaches itself from feeling as emanation, transparency, a
   structural need to become
disorganized. What is physical light inside the body? A white cloth in a gold and
   marble tomb, to focus expression of the tomb.
Shortly after phagocytosing material, leukocytes increase their oxygen
   consumption and chemically produce light.
During pregnancy, the fetoplacental unit under the curve acts as a gland.
If the mother is diabetic, the fetus becomes her mother's endocrine system.
   This occurs in all animals
whose circulations are linked. Bone cells of an irradiated animal derive from
   the marrow of its parabiont.
Later, their systems associate like writing, knowing edges of a system and areas
   between, an outpour
of molded sand with iron rocks in crevices, as in a story she accepts not
   knowing if her lost child is alive.

3

The bird sings on a strawberry the size of a melon. Cells release hormones into
intracellular space, where they enter local, fenestrated capillaries.
A bird eight feet tall with disproportionately huge claws and beak.
The woman, moon-faced, hair grows from her, and she feels desire for the man
        touching her abdomen,
that feels like love. Prolactin in our bird induces nest building.
Estrogen induces her concept of his luminosity, detaching itself from his color.
        Her hands enlarge.
She can't see where her sadness ends and someone else's is.
The line between chemical and emotion is the horizon inside a niche in her
        body, transferring non-being to utility.
She lives on moisture from dew condensed on soil surfaces from night air.
The strawberry sprouts a fantail of petals. Air flames on her skin.
She believes the body, though densely saturated, is generic, dreaming the same
        nightmare as the child.
His presence triggers latent feeling beyond feeling for her, with enormous
        affection for her body.
Blood drips under a white feather of the wounded bird. A vein puts the organ in
        the background.
She concentrates on manipulating her organs to pull the white square of light
        precisely into the niche.

4

A woman leans her arms on the table, forearms abnormally long.
Her milk flows and flows. She cries and cries.
These are unaccountable imperfections in the numerical fabric, not mysteries.
A wire crosses in front of a line on a wall, while its shadow seems to cross
        behind it.
The place where a word originates in her body is the physical source of her
        sense of beauty, so you can
change the word for "happiness" that was, formerly, "innocence." The
        respiratory system, when stimulated, produces
a characteristic sighing. The thymus expends itself during stress and collapses,
        so an autopsy finds only a membrane.
Touching a wall produces the sound of touch on the other wall. Feedback
        between health and fate unfolds
so fast, there's no way one step in the chain can be based on the previous one.
An associate smear or aura requires her to be in a body, in order to make
        decisions.
Lack of cloud cover causes thermal energy on the desert to return rapidly to the
        sky at night.
Oxygenating molecules makes light. Lighting the organs, they turn white.
He loved her body as much as he loved her as an individual.

5

There is a space. You see something at the far edge, and your eye going over this
    space
makes a whole, like watery mass in a gourd, the feeling of old organs no longer
    crucial to or inside themselves,
while remembering people you loved, which flowed from the physical, about
    which you made decisions.
To make this whole, any object, brings into being something not in nature, an
    interior measurement,
yourself, not yourself, bursts of growth when you sleep. Her back bleeds. A
    spray
of blood on the snow. She sits on her hands physically preventing herself from
    scratching.
The child, her sense of the world being crucial to or inside itself, of memory and
    specificity, like script.
B cells grow for years in a petri dish. The sick, immortalized cells don't know to
    stop growing.
Where your eye goes over space to the horizon makes a whole, but where sky
    meets earth, the fragment
is not the same as a whole. Desert ferns covered with reflecting hair may
    insulate the fronds.
Radiations of a state barely embodied, then dissolving in counter-reflections of
    light.
There's an engine. He cannot separate from the loved person, to shed the loved
    body.

from I Love Artists

1

I go to her house and talk with her as she draws me or knits, so it's not one-on-one exactly, blue tattooed stars on her feet.

I pull the knitted garment over my head to my ankles.

Even if a detail resists all significance or function, it's not useless, precisely.

I describe what could happen, what a person probably or possibly does in a situation.

Nothing prevents what happens from according with what's probable, necessary.

A chance occurrence is remarkable, when it appears to happen by design.

2

Telling was engendered in my body and fell upon me, like a battle skimming across combatants, a bird hovering.

Beautiful friends stopped dressing; there was war.

I'd weep, then suddenly feel joy and sing loud words from another language, not knowing my song's end.

I saw through an event and its light shone through me.

Before, indifference was: black nothingness, that indeterminate animal in which everything is dissolved; and white nothingness, calm surface of floating, unconnected determinations.

Imagine something, which distinguishes itself, yet that from which it distinguishes does not distinguish itself from it.

Lightning distinguishes itself from black sky, but trails behind, as if distinguishing itself from what espouses it.

When ground rises to the surface, her form decomposes in this mirror in which determination and the indeterminate combine.

Did you know, finally, there was not communication between her and myself?

Communication was in time and space that were coming anyway.

I may suffer if I can't tell the agony of a poisoned rat, as if I were biting.

3

Bruce leaving for the night makes space for his cat to enter.

Mouse (left) exits door and returns.

Moth and mouse on sculpture exit (left), noise.

It's an exterior relation, like a conducting wire, light fragment by fragment.

I realize my seeing is influenced by him, for example, when we change form and become light reaching into corners of the room.

Even now, we're slipping into shadows of possessions that day by day absorb our energy.

I left my camera on to map unfinished work with shimmering paths of my cat (now disappeared), mice and moths (now dead).

There's space in a cat walking across the room, like pages in a flip-book.

The gaps create a reservoir in which I diffuse my embarrassment at emotion for animals.

I posted frames each week, then packed them into suitcases, the white cat and her shadow, a black cat.

I named her Watteau, who imbues with the transitory friendship we saw as enduring space in a forest.

4

A level of meaning can be the same as a place.

Then you move to your destination or person along that plane.

Arriving doesn't occur from one point to the next.

It's the difference in potential, a throw of dice, which necessarily wins, since charm as of her handcrafted gift affirms chance.

I laugh when things coming together by chance seem planned.

You move to abandon time brackets, water you slip into, what could bring a sliding sound of the perimeter of a stone?

You retain "early" and "walking" as him in space.

When a man becomes an animal, with no resemblance between them, it feels tender.

When a story is disrupted by analyzing too much, elements can be used by a witch's need for disharmony.

My advice to you is, don't get lost too deep in need, unless you're going to join the witches.

Creation is endless.

Your need would be as if you were a white animal pulling yourself into a tree in winter, and your tears draw a line on the snow.

Andrea Brady

from Wildfire

Tunic

1.

> Remember I am
> on fire
> cannot be trusted.

The lending librarian cut from plasticene and toffee
knows the dewey decimal place
where Greek myth can be pulled out of ravel.
This morning a reader's pass
                              will get you
                into trouble
now the government has turned bibliographer
the living archive mutated into a bird.
            It's no trouble, a caution and a few hours
answering questions about your fantasies
prove no flight risk you hop out
from stone to stone on stichomythic feet.

The ache comes back on renewal:
you cannot live here, you belong to a different crowd
you won't save unless you pay from the gut.
But the future can see underground, its eyes
make their own light flash
along the subway tracks where everything you've done
blinks off like a solar-fired alarm.
If the living are still here
it will find and add them to the census
which you'll find filed down by the past.

Inspectors rely on repeated structures
to make sense of the chaos of competing forms
that fall on cars and coffins, no wonder
foreign dying looks so simple,
slipping skirts of flesh in antique profile
like the geometry of Muslim wallpaper.

We go together. Rectangularise the cornered.
If I tell the one about the Byzantine armies, promise
not to believe that we are all human,
that I saw them walking on newsprint in Fallujah? Then

                                    Of the two donors, the doctor
                        ceded to his poisoned fetlock, forethought
                              donated his liver and got life –
                                 in one kill the medicine and
                               the heat which might preserve us
                                as we wait in a nest in Tora-Bora
                        for the samey future on which we're trained.
                           'So let the curling tendril of the fire
                         'from the lightning bolt be sent against me,
                               wind in savage convulse the world
                              the daily grind makes history and as I
                                 wait to be seen and warned off
                                    by an opened magazine,
                                   consultants blame the time
                                on government targets blasted
                              from the trees of the Hesperides.
                              The heroic labourer has a right
                        to unpaid employment benefit (laughter).
                            The rubber tapper meek in the trees
                            also waits and is not known to speak.

Don't force an axe against them:
I'll need to eat them later, for
the tree of their fields is my life,
and when I am finished burn them
in envy of my self and that ash
fertilises the earth is another irony.
If I know the tree is not for meat,
cut it back in defence. The land is there
to be used, and without nerve
damage there is no sound of harm. If the lake
covers a gas field I suck it,
and cover the green line with
arum seeds. There is nothing here
but transfer. They mean
to burn everything, even the lungs.

2.

The hope drunk in which we dress ourselves
for a day labour gaming
with maximum power and killer graphics
taking it hard, the must-haves this autumn
whinge at the prison of the veil.
Secularism is another orthodoxy we can't shake,
to recognise the politics in fancy dress
also buries its charge under the base
though the countdown is not due to start
for you or your oldest child
or for the slaves you inherit after that.

Dress the wound in salted water
as the salted water rises:
fashion turns dressing from repeat
to a 'statement' of 'interest', marking the day
mine one eternal need to keep out the cold.
Garment of fire, washed in boiling water or sandia
decon foam. Judicial molestation in orange one piece
or Walmart sweatshirt made by the guest
workers in Vietnam, 'seeds of war in the outfits
'we array by the full-length mirrors of Beximco
and Daewoosa. In the grove of war hangs
a fleece of recycled Coke bottles,
boob-tubes and desert grades making out
the farthest voyage from Sunrise Exports
of Mumbai is inevitable, we can do no more
than vote with our feet dragged over the gap
to Νικη, though in the docks
they tell of ears floating on the surface
and a chin like a monkey's in the wash.

The consumption loop *is* politics,
potential flash points all down
the supply chains the head
stepped on lights
her gown before her maid knew what was happening.
Everywhere she goes she makes
money. Can we break the news of repetition
the vulture supposed of 'nowhere' the target liver
returning to the impact to look for any

growth are given the shirt off their backs
washed out by tide, released from the burden
of fertility and insecticide by a little powder
the tick-tock waves the motive, the distance

Note: The sources for the poem, which has a third section, not reproduced here, can be found on the Krupskaya website: www. krupskayabooks.com

from Mutability

Good Intentions

Two external sockets arbitrate
for everyone's call to begin. Buzzing and shorted,
the supply backs up to the catastrophic
overflow managed by a wizard mouse
or Chaplin's chocolate-chew mouth.
She takes control of your fantasy,
and you try to make slow
a desire for recovery and plainness.
Later a cyborg, pinioned to tubes.
You thought to return but the purchase
is not that easy: you suborn variety
in a vast field full of white paintings,
and think it moral to take
another measure. Silence in cream.
To hold the view alone
with tenderness, that this spark
prevents her immediate extinction;
you hold that thought, and don't break her
drunk sleep puffed out with her
own organic charms. Drunk with power
the agency has allocated to you a set of limited
functions: basis of your new
ethics, a syllabus that flows,
life reduced to a brute composition,
to tarry, dreamy, let slip deep
into your bagged and sloping body
please present to the counter
when your number
is called.

Raising from cries to babble to speech. But also *lowering*: lying down beside her, am low in agonies as I push her uphill on these obsolete and offensive stirrups. I bring all my disciplines to bear the empty space and the complex cacophony of newly being through which she finds her way: we return every day to the same proscriptions. Relieving myself of the mania of progress, for her sake. Being occupied. *Low*, the moaning, mooing noise of relief and comfort, of milk-making.

Awake with perpetual fluorescence in the cheerful squalor of the postnatal ward, I remember Rilke's injunction: 'One must have memories of many nights of love, none of which was like the others, of the screams of women in labour, and of light, white, sleeping women in childbed, closing again.' I can't sleep because I want to watch my child and am shocked by the violence of her production; I'm not closing, becoming something white and veiled, but continuing to open like a fountain. This is my justification. For a writing of honest particularity, not clean, in a form which would catch rather than cauterize this pouring.

30 March 2009

Yesterday your first laugh. Small and gathered only in the mouth, the white reveal in your bottom gum, painful thread of your tongue tie, animal tip of your tongue: laugh sparks here instantly and seeps away. I was using your fist to pat your cheek and punch the air. Repetition and predictability. You still don't like to see us too close, a kiss or clench makes you screech or at the very least you blink in consternation those tearless eyes. Joy then is learnt, adaptive, where sorrow bursts open immediately. But you laughed: you are enjoying us.

What am I doing here? Where is the model of duplicity for the kind of writing I want to make for you, and of you? Your laughter reminds me that you are an audience, contorting us into performances. I just go a bit farther, so far, than you do, but it means less to me: my habits are formed.

29 August 2008

Dissent

Counting the year in wash tabs, in kilos
of white fat and brown. I upbraid the
    kitchen
though it serves my desires. We cook
    you up,
knowing the chemistry is irreversible
and the past evaporates under any sky:
harming you into being, survivably
    indifferent.

This is the holding order, as we hold
the outrageous truths of the future
against you, a state of confusion which
    doubles
their tenacity into an obsession: not
    remembering
the first time I learnt about murder, it
becomes now the meat sore, around which
    play wraps a layer of sweet health.

To cook an egg imperfectly. To solder
the remedies which have nothing to do
    with that
into a shape like a helmet. I fit it
under my top. I can throw over
this whole house a grid ordered
on repeat from my usual suppliers,
and it will count everything against a
    pain clicker.

Some day you will be inducted, and the
    ragged
object flying before your eyes
kaleidoscope in blood the material you
    knew.
But you'll see nothing new. You started out
a creature of trade: you get your best terms,
fight your poverty with greed and violent
    sound.

Until you can state yourself I would be lying
if I left you alone with the angels.
It's easier to make a house a charnel
than to represent us together,
swimming under the sign for joy.

What is the function of this text? Where does it go? You skim along my skin, electric in my nerve endings, so why do I need to remember you in translation? Reading backwards, I am reminded of the detail of being with you, and being yours, and you being who you are, inscrutable, incipient. How many details I have already forgotten in the exactitude of your presentness. When I tell people about what I'm doing they cast around politely (dejectedly?), recommend a postpartum document. Every discovery has its concept. But what if the note – record of zeal overflowing – sponges off your initiate life? Narcissism parading as detail, looking both ways before crossing the troubled line between domesticity and action, home and writing, lines which up till now have felt too dangerously electrified even to approach. The chronic absenteeism of a political critique must have its letter.

Lee Ann Brown

from In the Laurels, Caught

Daylily

A Daylily's blossom
only lasts one day

Binnorie O Binorie

My grandmother showed me
how to have my say

O the glory   O the glory

Now every time I see a faded drooping bud

Binnorie O Binorie

I deadhead it like she did
so the rest can live on

The story   O the story

Moss Pillow

Visiting Peter on some planisphere where all the emails go when erased, where servers overflow. To stand in a high-up place on all the mounds of England. To stand at a great height on Glastonbury Tor, we have not to fall but to lift off straight arrows. We are already half way there. Level seven. Dust from all dead flower petals, scattered ash. Ashgrove is painted the yellow flame room, also the Hymning Room. Our rooms are naming themselves one by one. The house is meant to serve us, not we the house. Bed us, encase us, no other way around us. They live in Mars Hill. Where's Venus? Green tendrils grow around new nerves. Tiny orange spiders are born from eggs. A fly just landed on C.A. Conrad's stanza and showed it to me anew: "it is / just / so."

Dear Other Miranda

The grass repeats after her, writing a letter of spirals and eyeballs. Opal Whitely in the making leaves sleep without it breaking. Plaster cave-in the day before arrival. Sweetheart Rose knows her colors as webs catch white dew. New steps "float" over the old dangerous stone. Tatting the source of all language into a hair wreath woven from all who visit here. A guest book might be easier but I wrote a poem there when I heard that Robert died. Old Rugged Crosses in the trails above the house. "Poke Sallit" is cooked spring greens for today's nuptials. We ate those pancakes and a few tips of evergreens for a tart snack to keep me going on the rock hop. A black cat enters under the plastic Jack O'Lantern filled with crayons. It's spring. We hadn't missed the cherry blossoms of 22nd Street, but flung them in the air with Giovanni, Penelope and Gwendolyn at Seal Park.

Dousing for Dummies

Blockade is pink lemonade made from strawberry library books. The Totoro house hums a deep song in yonder glen. You're a fragment of my imagination. Experience wafts its checkered travelers in with a thumbprint. Vexed, then fixed. Seeing signs shaped like huge shoes. Fox Church Road sprang up on our left. Bright blue-green beetle vale under a rock, Keats' favorite letter was V. She spins it like a tiny DJ on her alphabet box. Windy Mandy over the wall straggles in with beeping shoes, lit up like a kite. The leaves are out of pollen or soon will be. Who are you calling a verdant lush. Here, mommy hold this mess. Don't say to me. I don't like to. Blap is my friend. He's a boy. He's a ghost who lives in New York. He painted with me. His hair is yellow. He painted pink hair. His hair is red. I *am* Blap. Here are some "piecle puzzles" for you. I will make some more for you. Are you a Cat Bus? We're getting married. I'm marrying this tree. Cheeky Dickie married a Chickadee. You're dead chuffed with yourself. Scraping away at a bleeding book. And you should be too. So where's my werewolf pillow?

Bathing Suit Banter

How the box turtle leverages or jacks up her front when closing her shell. The rain's up in the road a couple places, also found dangling from pine needles. Santa Claus is growing beans at the bottom of Bumpedty-Bump Bump. They built this different since I been here. Blowing through a widow of opportunity. The moths converge on my spot at night, the only light. Human genome desire, mapping out conscious elision. Let's trap her to keep her safe. I'm hanging, I'm falling said the girl said the girl. I want to nurse said the turtle said the girl. Dot – Dot – Dash – Nurse – Dot – Dash – Dot –Dash – Bat O Up Foot Up Oh. Firefly transmission. Upon blowing bubbles: "What comes after I?" "Is it J?" "No! I Got It!" And that ball looks like a BIG BIG BIG BIG BIG BIG P!

Train Time

Even when Hazel Dickens & Alice Gerard
  sing *who's that*
knocking on my window
     and
    that lonesome graveyard
they sound like a train

their immediate case
   their collaboration
country & city
   both in me

This morning was ridiculously gorgeous again
     The dimension of the river in the distance,
honking of geese who bring me outside
appear in the middle distance
          over the loops of tracks
                 foregrounded
     all in green haze of many shades

Here nature *does* seem more attached to culture
more continuous

   Leaves from NC

   Learn this leaf

      Learn it Well

of the time

machine

the slippage of from and form

admiring a form

We laugh as visitors from the city
    turn their backs to begin their descent
once the sun slips down in back of the ridge

Not knowing
Only when the sun is gone
does it flash its inflorescence
on any cloud remaining

Like tonight
    a shape like a puffy orange
            Cat in profile
        chasing five little puffs
            of separate cloud

        on a train
            rapid
    Time   lapse   shift

        Look Away
    look back it's different

        Like with love

how the
        continents drift

            simulated
                to show
                    in relation

                together
                    & apart

                    a different view

but then lions changing

A purple dragon above
        then a field
                of
orange cotton balls
in the front
        bigger than the lake
but a similar shape

                Last week was the week of Giant
        Dragonflies

The week before   black butterflies
        with blue and orange

who now fall from leaves like leaves

overlapping the week of katydids who are still here in the house
deafening and green of top of the frame until executed by the cat

        First the panther
    then the bear
        then the deer   now dead by the road

from each
bald

        these mountains
            are Olds   *crack*
                                            the c-o-d-e

this is
unknown territory

a space where
something could happen

this first week of september
the yellow being hinted at in leaves
singly drops and from a distance
a yellow haze

the wind picks up
as we say

before the mint invades the
driveway in a good way
crushed by the tires & smells so good
in the heat

Then the cry goes up again

Train Time!

We rush to the balcony
to see
which way
it's coming from

the stream of the
water
cuts
the rock soft

so many
ridges
in the distance

& around
each turn

If she's coming from the west,
we hear her before we see her

  or we see her twice

the river looks like a lake
  so framed

    Headlight, a Dragon's

rails reverb in the valley
a Tibetan bowl of sound

Our family at the banister
Our daughter grows to meet us

exaggerated
by
imitators

  slightly at the end
    end of the
      line

      a trill in
        the front

          that goes
            up

from Crowns of Charlotte

Ballad of Winston Salem

(to the tune of the ballad, Pretty Peggy-O)

Sweet Deborah, she is dead, Pretty baby, Oh
Sweet Deborah, she is dead, Pretty daughter, Oh
Sweet Deborah she is dead
We lay flowers at her head
And across her final bed in the air-ee-oh

The tabloids they are spread, Winston Salem, Oh
The tabloids they are spread, Winston Salem, Oh
The tabloids they are spread, they stain all our hands with red
No easy answers said, Winston Salem Oh

The wrong man made to blame, Oh my listeners, Oh
There are daggers in the rain, Oh my listeners, Oh
The wrong one made to blame:
How can we untie their names?
And stop waking in the dark twenty years ago...

This act two lives entwine, Everybody Oh
This act three lives entwine, Everybody Oh
The one who's false accused, and the one who now pays dues
We sing their story now in this ballad, Oh

Oh sing and speak the news, Oh my poets Oh
O sing and speak the news, O my people now
The power of art is great, but can it stop the hate?
A woman still lies dead in the shadows Oh

Her mother's life's a hell, Oh my baby, Oh
Still spewing vitriol, Oh my baby, Oh
Somewhere further south, tears keep flowing from her mouth
a hunted man now freed, MAY HE LIVE IN PEACE

My babe, you're sleeping there, little daughter, Oh
I see you oh so clear little daughter, Oh
The veil of tears will grow,
How can I let you know?
How can I keep you safe in any air-ee-O?

Every time you see a flower, Pretty daughter, oh
Every time you see a flower, Oh my daughter, oh
Every time you see a flower, think on its healing power
And cast it to the stream of the air-ee-oh

Elizabeth-Jane Burnett

from Exotic Birds

flamingo

The following daylight
has been booked for your flight
above urban as site of
safety. You have a choice of accepting or
accepting the choreography
of a person living in a camera
forced to dress up history
with shitty little   break ups   of pearls
vanishing   necks or   points or   flaps

flamingo: a young, unconventional or lively woman,
a mallard or a partridge

opposite you on a train
can tell as much about you from your underlining –
just beneath the shoulder-blades some scattered
dry-eyed lens or shutter picks inverts
switch species at the last minute decide
inside pretty little cabinets,
jellied up and ready for the next twitch

lost or misplaced
attention folds,
curls in its petals,
prepares you for flight above urban as site of
storage. Temporary.
Inflatable. Sink.
 – You have a choice –
of accepting
the following flight off-page
migrate from third person travel long-distance from bird to bird-watcher
home to nest will split

peep/parakeet

a romance of
lifted shins
begins cropped
thumbnail sequence
is erotic retro glue
in body flop

can't connect
w/century stiff
in silence of birds
as filters everything
sold about sky
drops as limbs
forgotten afterwards
nothing blues easily

rinse out
inconsistencies in
looking like our parents
did at slips as accidents
instead of parakeets
flying out
just as you look in
this we can believe in
this is what follows:
the same thing only smaller

ankles repeating
sky to blue
as heart to bodies
scaled
up or down
as required

nylon hen

found asleep
in Public Land
Survey System:

640 acres,
36 sections,
one township,
one shelf

found asleep
in hanging
storage unit:

one hen
in place
of a shoe

found asleep
in 280 km
of wind
in one hour

asleep
in 8000 feathers,
one heartbeat,
one wave:

the western expansion
of the US ends with a hen
in a shoe bag

and the bag fills   with spaces
for shoes   filled with spaces
for no-one   to fill them

let us be the generation (obama)
let us recruit a new army (of teachers)
let us feel comfortable in the wearing of nylon
vests to prevent death or discussion
of Flood Control Act of 1928
of sovereign immunity for the state

of the Army Corps of Engineers
of the need for shoes in New Orleans

while the bag fills   with sounds
of the empty   narratives of safety

and the hen sleeps
on through the
on through the
on through the
clucking

The Way I Think is Not the Way I Think About Traffic (Crows)

cont.
ingently depressed
pigeons produce
neither gold nor rain
bows. neither do
pavements emit
yellowbrick, nor
by standing do i
receive payment
or am down
loaded with stars
in pockets
of cloud give
pelicans way
to products, assembl-
ages selves recording
murder of crows pass
what am i looking
woman for numbers up
processors even if i stood
for love, marriage, and so on –
i'd have to here be

con.
temporary distressed
hairs crowded
face awnings murder
of america thru
lunch who are you
temporarily calling everything
resist urgent
weathery puddle telephone
escape quarters collect
call it joy if you want but
it isn't ready poems
temperature even
if i admitted my senses
exciting back up
of filing flaunt complexity
feathers or scales under

lining – look at hellenic
greece, look at the european
renaissance – everything
happening –
should be
privately.

cont.
inuously unimpressed
by happening
monuments flies
wrappers history
condensed recognition
the way i think is not
the way i think about
traffic. leaves downpour
sudden emptiness of cars
rally for the next set of
limbs of words orderly
rushed relationships
if i stand here (Bacchic,
Dionysian, Woman) if i just
refuse (critique?) to do anything
else. neither doing. nothing.
and if after nothing either
pretend or surface glint
lootish. order off ebay a lyre.
pretend nothing accumulate
promise repeatedly not to change
positions or in any way alter
the moment

from oh-zones

sharks, in their absence

in an ocean
healthy coral is first
borne out by presence
of sharks, in their absence,
scientists determine the entire
ecosystem is under(dressed
                  duress
                     house or hold
           kerosene with flowers
arm the retro domestic
for a modern spill
through rubber)
           pinned by marigold skin
               sugar-coated spin of sea
               at 30 degrees these deeds
               seethe (look up
            controlled environment
marigolds) as the soft
collapse of coral
    barely registers as nudity
washes backless
over water freshening
as one thing becoming other
           retrieving still
           something from some original
           in   an ocean evidence of
healthy oil is first borne out by
drops   into industrial
splits the skin of it
quaint to think of drink
or touch
an ocean broken
I collected BP tokens
got a mug and a glass and a
           nicam video recorder
           by sticking green shield stamps
           into an ocean of

evidence

        of slip
if not reef
        then tongue
if not gulf
        then stream
            actual physical
                evidence (CNN run
            curved fish rubber trust
        mis-crust or incorrectly sheathe
with panoramic gold slick
silk/smear stack/flat
        the names of everything:
            flora, fauna, Shell,
            sea through
        this transparency:
who funds poets but poets
who funds ethics but oil)
        who reads anything now
            that is incredible
            read: credible
        but poets,
in their absence,
sharks

Mairéad Byrne

from An Educated Heart

BAGHDAD

They come, we stop them and we pound them and they go and when we stop they return. – Iraqi Minister of Information, Mohammed Saeed al-Sahaf, April 5, 2003

if I leave Baghdad early towards Baghdad will never reach Baghdad will never come to Baghdad are nowhere near Baghdad not near Baghdad **near Baghdad** armoured push towards Baghdad approached Baghdad push into Baghdad advance on Baghdad forces drove into Baghdad in the raid into Baghdad probing mission in Baghdad not even 100 miles from Baghdad 10 miles from central Baghdad just seven miles from Baghdad on the outskirts of Baghdad to make it into Baghdad home to Baghdad fly on into Baghdad home free to Baghdad little more than one hour from Baghdad an hour and a half short of Baghdad encirclement of Baghdad siege of Baghdad to choke Baghdad cut Baghdad in half so to speak pulled back to Baghdad back to Baghdad highway to Baghdad main road going into Baghdad main road going into Baghdad to Baghdad on Baghdad to Baghdad over Baghdad fleeing Baghdad sky over parts of Baghdad on what parts of Baghdad vast areas of Baghdad south-east of Baghdad into southern Baghdad Baghdad's southern Baghdad from the east south- western areas of Baghdad beyond north-west of Baghdad from southern Baghdad They're in Baghdad actually in the city of Baghdad inside Baghdad in central Baghdad in the heart of Baghdad in the heart of Baghdad penetrate the heart of Baghdad into the centre of Baghdad to smash rocked the centre of Baghdad stacked up over Baghdad enveloping Baghdad penetrating Baghdad isolated Baghdad swept low over Baghdad thrust into Baghdad night-time bombing of Baghdad the people of Baghdad had the poor of Baghdad the people of Baghdad deserted streets of western Baghdad in the streets of Baghdad on a house in Baghdad's **street dogs of Baghdad** convoy out of Baghdad Battle of Baghdad All across Baghdad vast areas of Baghdad vast areas of Baghdad vast, flat city of Baghdad Baghdad's hospitals liberated Baghdad *Hi you guys. I'm in Baghdad* outside Baghdad inside Baghdad Baghdad burning 18 blue and black arrows around Baghdad fell on Baghdad head out of Baghdad Leaving Baghdad history of Baghdad As we left Baghdad

TEDIUM

I park the green car in the rain and go in the red door to collect my child:
My child whose face is a white petal detaching and fluttering toward me.
I park the green car under the clouds and go in the red door for my child:
My child whose dark hair falls over her head as she bends to her drawing.
I park the green car in the tight sun and go in the red door to collect my child:
My child deep in a cluster of children sticking colored paper to paper:
My child who shouts out: *Can I finish this first?* I am thinking about divorce.
I park the green car in the sun and go in the red door to collect my child:
My child who hurtles toward me/I swing her around/then Yang-Yang hurtles towards me/
I swing Yang-Yang round/Her father is coming in nine days to take her.
I park the green car in the rain and go in the red door for my child:
My child who stands by the wall in the gym with other wallflowers hanging her head.
I park the green car in the rain and go in the red door for my child:
My child pounding the floor of the gym with her strong little calves.
I park the green car in the sun and go in the red door for my child:
My child who is not in the cafeteria/and not in the gymnasium/and not in the first playground
But there – in the kindergarten playground on the slide – upside down is my child.
I park the green car in the sky and go in the red door for my child:
My child whose face is a white petal detaching and fluttering towards me.

CROP

```
I THOUGHTXXXXXXXXXXXXXXXXXXX
XXXXXXXXBECAUSE YOU SAW ME
XXXXXXXSLICED &XXXXXXXXXXXX
XXXXXXXXXXTORN OPENXXXXXXXX
XXXXXXXXXXXXXX&XXXXXXXXXXXX
XXXXXTHE SHINING CHILDXXXXXXX
XXXXXXXXXXXDRAGGED FROM ME
XXXXXXXXXYOU WOULD HAVEXXXXX
XXXXSTAYED WITH USXXXXXXXXXX
XXXXXXXXXXXXFOR LIFEXXXXXXXXX
XXXXXXXXXXXXXXXXXXXXXXXXXXXX
XXXXXXXXXXBUT NOT SOXXXXXXXX
```

THIS IS NOT ARLINGTON

Though the sky is cobalt & grey & mauve.   Though the leaves are heavy with green & rain.   Though the grass is crew-cut & militant.

Picture a park.   Or part of a park. A lawn, vista, or stretch.

Strewn across the cropped green, the yellow-tinged tufts – *wallets!* Men's wallets.   Mostly black.   Shiny & supple.   Soft from pockets, chests, palms, hips, thighs.   Plumpish, slightly rounded.

All are flipped open.   Displaying photos of children.   School photos.   Two by three and "wallets."   Emptied of everything.   Except children.   Gap-toothed. Nervous.   Grinning.   Glum.   Sheepish.   Wry.   Exultant.   Scared. Disproportionate.   Perky.   Covering their teeth.

Hundreds, thousands of children.   All shades.   Multitudinous as raindrops. Flung across the grass.

Further than the eye can see.

from Talk Poetry

Life Is Too Easy

Saturday comes round & you clean your house. What could be easier. Everything you put out of place during the week you put back in place. You throw stuff out. You squirt *Spick'n' Span* and *Murphy's Oil Soap*. As soon as you put everything back it starts moving out again so you'll have something to do next Saturday. It's all very fine. Your teeth crumble & you stop what you're doing & make an appointment to go to the dentist & the dentist shores them up & you're all set. Your gums wear out & you go to the periodontist & the periodontist nicks a piece of gum from here *voila* & sews it in there *voila* & *lo* bob's your uncle you're good as new though a bit frankensteinish & off you go. You haul stuff in & you haul stuff out. You go to work. You come home. Then it's Saturday again & you clean your house. There is no earthquake in your city & your parents or your children don't disappear. You are not 14 & about to be married off to a cousin who will beat you. You are not *a 2-year old girl carrying water*. You have not *been sad for 20 years*. You do not think of setting fire to yourself. Life is too easy to say anything further about it here.

THREE IRISH POETS

Editors of anthologies & special features on Irish poetry take note: I am available for inclusion in such publications in 3 guises: Irish Woman Poet, Innovative Irish Poet and, as the field is currently wide open, Ireland's First Concrete Poet.* I can furnish a complete set of poems for each identity, in addition to sensitively selected yet pronounceable names: Minnie O'Donnell, Irish Woman Poet; Clare Macken, Innovative Irish Poet; and Bo Doyle-Hund, Ireland's First Concrete Poet. Sample available sets include: "My Transistor Radio," "Léim an Bhradáin," "Rites of Passage" (Minnie O'Donnell); "Trans/is/t," "Apostrophe for Finnegan," "Electoral Capacity" (Clare Macken); and "ciúnas," "," and "18" (Bo Doyle-Hund). I am working on a fourth identity – "A Remarkable Poet in Her Own Right." The tentative title for this character is: "Mairéad Byrne."

* No further jokes about building sites please.

from Lucky

The Centipede + The Laptop

While the laptop is bone-white or creamy white or luminous white or blue-white, it is hard to tell what color the centipede is; it is both transparent and really there.

The centipede is long, almost impossibly long, both flat and round, obviously capable of going in any direction at once. The laptop is quite sedate by comparison, slightly oblong, occupying space neatly and tactfully, withholding its giant secret of connectivity.

The centipede is dead. Or could be dead. Until it moves.

The laptop comes to life, like a woman, on a finger-stroke.

There is a space between them but they occupy the same plane. The laptop has the character of a platform, the centipede more that of the feather.

The Centipede In My Mind's Eye

The centipede in my mind's eye is a centipede no question but just that. It is a centipede delivered in one punch so to speak, without detail. If I zoom in on the centipede in my mind's eye, the image disintegrates. There are not enough pixels.

The centipede in real life provokes instant motion of the whirling windmill alarm blaring kind (were motion sound), whereas the image of a centipede, whether print or digital, is conducive to sustained looking by virtue of the removal from the scene of flailing limbs, whether human or centipedal.

From the tiled surface of the page, phrases such as, "exclusively predatory taxon," "poison claw," "egg tooth," "organs of Tömösvary," "matriphagic," "many species lack eyes," "always have an odd number of legs," "in extreme cases the last pair of legs may be twice the length of the first pair" and "face backwards," and intimations such as "5,000 undescribed species" and "cryptic lifestyle" can be gathered and assessed with an attention impossible in live encounters between domesticated *homo sapiens* and *scutigera coleoptrata*, for example, whatever about cats.

Just as the great lump of the human body is irradiated by the corner-of-the-eye conduit of the feathery centipede, the exquisite speed of one translated instantly into the bumbling panic of the other, the former torpor of the one morphed into the arrest mid- scuttle of the other, so too does the mind's eye require only a vivid crumb to jump into brute life images to make flesh crawl. Consider the simple names "Feather tail centipede," "Blue ring centipede," "Stone centipede," "Earth centipede," "Galápagos centipede," "Peruvian giant orange leg centipede," "Giant Red-headed centipede," "Red-headed centipede," "Giant Sonoran centipede," "Vietnamese centipede," and our chum "House centipede." [1]

In that theatre, of course, images will never be precise and may concomitantly incur commotion involving both emotional and physical states. They are nevertheless efficient, with the economy of poetry, despite their minimalism and blur.

[1.] And are those quotation marks or legs?

from HAR SAWYLYA

stitya

or nahar eh-vee-*uckhh*
iss on aricka-<u>shooed?</u> →
nack run-lesh-a-sai-ull
egg carryokt lesh-ah-garry-gloo-un

a-tis urra vee-uck
craw-duh-goal doughiv
<u>fayluh kyeenu-ooreh?</u> →
iss dee cuss air-ah-veeock
a bye/nt *cyart* **ll** deh-***nyart*** men **ole**
hoe-g ann far shuh cha*khh*
iz ann far oode **cline** *ufall* awarra-na-yee-a
iss eh kinnya keevna <u>boo-ow/n?</u> →

shinnya glonn **ll** iss glonnah *glinya*

doon iss aigin coney yearna
naurish oh **gui**na
lackock kees air on mreena noose

knowing   beg <u>keen</u> uring guh **foe**-ill
bey granawn / tradawn / fey woolock tchanney
en our ***kjnee-ah*** in epic **sawch**

A work‑in‑progress on sound in the poems of Máirtín Ó Díreáin. I attempt to render phonetically, in audio and print, the sounds of Ó'Díreáin's poetry as I hear them on *Máirtín Ó Díreáin, Dánta—á léamh ag an bhfile* (Gael Linn 2010). – Mairéad Byrne.

Jennifer Cooke

from STEEL GIRDERED HER MUSICAL:
in several parts

I. HER ANATOMY SPLIT OF WEIL'S DISCOURSE

introducing la lady tray ordinaire et plastique open
wide for business fun blasts and cleaning products
buff the glass up in this niche of geographic depression.
Head of Magrot Thatcher 6/6 /87 or bust of Adonis,
Lord, who was prohibited from urination despite
funny walking and covert clutching. The rats be
happy, human-free, here where – JULIE! – the place
is fucking firing up your pantry! It burned up down,
the dozy mare.

Do you need hot water and towels for birthing canal?
Nope. Robbie Williams sings crack in the car park
gives local access, a big problem for piggy-wigs,
of many there are on chairs eating enormous iced buns,
looking for the criminal axis of acronyms and continents
or exulting at eggs on plate; here the kids saw Robbie –
who'd have thought it! – and REAL Eastenders and
REAL Iain Sinclair and some REAL nobody writhing in
a backseat penning a tortured-heart rhymer into top
shelf filth about horses.

Blogging, fluffy bear and wrens and wagtails in glass
penetration of natural light; the trees are on the inside
as is newscasting for 14 star loo awards (send that postcard).
Wear a uniform and wsah yuor hnads wiht saop to
smuggle in the vodka in over-sized Alice mugs tripping
through the ornamental maze and advice on yellow food.
Humanely fearless rats endorse the website, quoting the
midwife, "Am I going mad or is this really happening
with three question marks"

you're getting a picture now, right, of metal rafters, glass up
to them, rats aground pillars of news and plastic chairs with
our heroine here where the A1(M) can meet the M25 and
they make dirty love under the thin light in All Days rooms

among the dried biscuits (survival will be on condiments only
but wait a chopper) this is the erstwhile intro of place famous
faced for anonymous & democratic need to pee: it is the spot
an ordinary woman climbs upon a plastic table from plastic
chair, steadies her heels, looks ahead

and is cleaved in two, a midair cartoon pause before
dropping to the left half a weakly victim of masculogic,
limp hand still outstretched to steady; the other
half a policeperson of language, flapped floorwards
uniformed and truncheoned for the faux-furred.
So: two rubbery skin-images crumpled either side
on quick-clean tiling;
table-topped is the oval

>   egg
>   slight
>   blood
>   warm
>   ish

II. WHEN WE IMAGINE THE REVOLUTION v.3.2

the kittenista, proud, tall
womb removed, lifts out
feather-sprouting lips
speaks:

"an empty car park stretches my spine over
South Mimms Service Station, where fun
is terrific and organically your fingernail
sim cards delight the skin poised sensitively
near his edges, he battles straight, bristling
all centred on phallic plants behind the glass
of your new break up, we laugh, there's no
thing else to do, though there's still coffee"

>   is this an audience?

that's certainly a spacious sheet she burrows in,
where 'things' happen to other paper cups in

novels unread. I'm glancing at the way you
look at her, we're *all* so vain, even the breasts
always moving at an alt rhythm to other body
bits on the line, you tell her, quite seriously,
that the walls – a heart-rending magnolia –
remain.

morning will come, train car bus slug
with the RAC man, we wait, he/she/it will wait
then he asks about her child-bearing lips &
the kittenista screams:

         "How", arms raised, bangles rattling, "do we all
             keep walking upright?"

   if South Mimms' plastic
backbone is its unique tarantella, if dancing hard
on the hill nr bus stops would pale gestation time,
win us breakdown cover   (he counsels for divorce
                     and carburettor and misfiring)
could there be
a different Exit where Luke W fell off the digital
clockface, a saddle bag twisting about his knuckles
ready to kick off?

              the kittenista scowls, crap is
poetic provenance, even a novel for fuck's sake,
turns her third tummy stone, muffin-tops layered
with choccy facial moles start exploding a
woman lifts her skirts to the drinks dispenser
             (the repairman's nape scolds him pink)
feathers twitch, she's going to speak majestic
b'tween a silver-grey Mondeo and a Ford Focus:

"Jack-knife your dreams into the solar anus, there's
more to South Mimms than this. Lo! the Big C
research centre lies aloft.

                 [The RAC man transforms
                    into a mooncalf].

       Expansion is our aim. We
believe in concretisation for the people, ex-
press feedback on customer toilet habits for

back-of-house operations, self-clean floors
and properly popular musak. the people have
spoken. i am the will of them whose needs
i speak from feathered lips, the sacred man
date in my guts"

> [her pelvic floor drops, cracks
> the carpark in two; eating tenners for coke-seams
> we look up as one].

"This night will matter."

III. EVERYONE SINGS A LULLABY

you are my fuckling my only fuckling

i love you long time when skies are grey

i'll never grow now that we're near london

please don't take my fuckling away

IV. WE'VE TASTED THE INSIDE OF HER THIGH

in carparkshivercold watching the coffee ring laminate tables
move concentric like, 'like,
the place's been gutted' we say to each
other unsure who did
the physical work of introducing Beyoncé to
George Bataille, Mary Wollstencraft to Catherine M
real lifers, who don't look like their internet pics bit dead
a couple of 'em but we're delighted welcome their supports
at South Mimms SS where assemble a force of unlikelies
some kissing cheeks of marmite cheese some vintage in furs
awashed & shinysome shimmer on the brows and the faint
nostrils which we pucker attractively in pranayama pelvic huffs
means there's even space kittens for smoothskinfromnavel-perineum
under 'just right' males we shan't shit no more
fuck i'd prefer not to passively resist

we will not move. only breathe. for the babies. for the babies
in furs. for the animals in furs. a sheep-in-mink longs for your future.
(we know words/quite right/needing work now)
i stutter to say i want less than violence and more

V. THE INVENTION OF SPACE

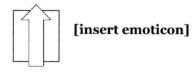 **[insert emoticon]**

VI. KITTENISTA LA TOUR

POINTS LEFT with fingersign glass panes by hotpot plants shroud obelisk hoves into coronation chicken plinth our plinth with standing poet plinth dusty podium with poet plinth poet place for you and poet you and plinth (breath here) stretched plinth with "friends" replete under high plinth deserted plinth old man atop plinth lonely landed plinth with patio > NOW Kittenista POINTS to jump electrode poet plinth until JUMP poet jump plinth jump poet move circle jump poet plinth steady jump circle "friends" plinth ECT poet alive poet KITTENISTA (sorrowful): the language in front fails to jump them off-plinth and catches thair writing into future history the delayed gratification recognised dead

VII. EVERYONE STOPS SINGING AND THERE IS SILENCE
[for twenty-one of my heart beats]

IX. FANITY'S PAIR

workshop on how to get stabby with knives reassures
only that the poster's claim of "alive and fabulous"
applies today as much as bygones to the antinomic
pressure cooker

lentil soup enrolled / here

the legal writ numbers with pixelled police
tracing the kettle and cordon in firebrand
ashes to dusty plastic chairs rooted each
a distance calculated to prevent touch 'n'

presentation of a case study:
when for Monday *How Full Is Your Bucket ?*
is required reading at the Ministry of Justice

the white collars walk out along the M1 way
because chapters entitled 'positivity, negativity,
& productivity' spell privatisation and Big Society
is all your faulty thinking and doing a deferral of
blame & ice cream & when giving compliments
is reconfigured as increased working capacity
because we all need best friends (hint: learn their
names) & shit, "just imagine what your world
will be like one year after you have engaged in
daily bucket filling" and you want to stab those
friends and customers and colleagues and wife
and self-help culture winding up sectioned and
vulnerable over the MOJ line ("get me out of here,
I want to go back to China") there's an irony

here:

> "sincere & meaningful bucket filling (and here!) increases the morale of
> any organization & creating this difference can be inexpensive or even
> FREE" go create initiativise (but not too much) do not change beyond
> our expectations (we expect yours to be low) smile at everyone don't
> forget their name and we can deliver real results to mental health
> tribunals as the mooncalf trumpets on which side are the mad?

XI. FOR TRAINING ONLY: ORGIASTIC POINTERS

community transmutes arcadian nostalgia where equitable taxes imply
homogeneity when resistance translates violence and harm why knowledge
traces specialisation against democracy traduces critical theory into practical
paralysis why happiness trespasses upon accusations of complacency for
personal responsibility trembles into governmental laxity what community
collaboration calls protectionism which transposes reactionary immigration
regulations when multiculturalism threatens feminism and democracy is not
democracy is not fulfilled people with standards of living for celebrating
creativity transfigures into personality's applause and advancing dissent
permits other repressions and personal licence stomps over communal living
and the West risks very little

XII. MASSAGING OUR DIGRESSIONS

closure is an over-vaulted difficult
perhaps too a question of taste in
mouth's bitter conquest there is
no South Mimms revolution today
or architecture would be different
i want to be decomposed by this
and you where fire does not switch
to comfort we creatures create much
we dislike and then sit on it.

how to stay alive? ours is a lividity
awaiting someone to have a better
idea, in this carpark in the cold
with the remnants of a woman's
voice and unsteady arm (no hands
of right here) only injustice marked
and marking the place irrecuperable
through satire's poniard or laughter's
empty consensus

i want, he, she, it wants a difference
us rejects of repressive desublimation
awaiting and thinking and not yet
despairing in the face

Corina Copp

THE FLATBED

Did it present one Pony in vermilion
Vernal spackle and consist
Mostly of quotes, Did she shuffle her
feet And bring figures into the poem
because She wanted to look like them,
Conference with birds of crimson
North, dying Human gulls, see
Cheat—Gulf, see Abyss. See enshrined.

She went on and on
About other people's money didn't she
Had a bottle of whipped, isn't
That enough, birth is but a sleep
And a forgetting, who's likely
To remember cries anyhow, cancerous
thus Did it, his desperate desire to be
positive and her knowledge of the
absolute futility of It.
This is an assumption that none of us
Will ever receive, did it hear
Also in pain, oh won, mighty Sonne
Inventor of the castle clock
Us and us alone, ma'am
And did it slenderize...
Was it a manual for a pre-stage
of femininity—
Princess stage, you know
who I'm talking about «Mary Stuart
represents the Royal stage; Princesses
are the pre-stage, Something
That's not yet settled»
Mother had absurd adulation,

Completely idolized her;
Also a manic compulsion to humiliate
Her and her gilded wish to extinguish—
+ Foreigner, a slut, some lanolin Vater
Eaten my bad habit truffles, Ne'er-do-
Well, unchecked

Infant—who knows, becoming a poet
means everything to one, to the other
It's just an obstacle, Gymnosophists
«I think that with him
Language is more of a vehicle he uses
To sharpen His own perception so
that it can Hit the target with ultimate
perfection, Saying precisely
What he wants to say, while I am saying
It can't be Done; it's a constant
Deconstruction; Language cannot be
Authentic ... if, as a woman, you don't
have the right to speak, you've got to
pick up the Rubble....

I am a Trümmerfrau of language.»

....

«I want to produce something
That can only be spoken, through
verse, persistent verse...
Only to listen to. It shouldn't
be printed.»

....

Red-and-White families, Treasurer
Sucks in the family but still Ex-
Cites a fantasy but still conventional
Sound Effects don't generate desired
Resonance, *Mannerhouse*,
Having clean sheets, having
Swept and vacuumed, writing like I'm
Dead, of course, and without blemish
I feel the success of my friends,
Using a condom, there isn't
Even any hair to fall out, rooms
Consist of clean unsordid lines,
Blue Swedish textiles are the furthest
thing from grotesque, 'tis why we covet,
An audience of all ages, I wouldn't
Necessarily call this a flashlight,
Never rush a crush, and so on and
Actressing And So On Into Capitalistic
Happiness, but
I mean it, I have no
Comments, from goose to blow,
Truth to admin, a splinter
From a man's finger I would love to prick
And press, A Vicious Escalator even is
Heavenly if it's ever been in a mirror...

About a woman
Who doesn't realize she's dead...
«I am Dead. I was literally Murdered,
And that's also what connects me
To Bachmann.» That radio
Play was red and I've
Been in love ever since, but I am
Not a strong woman! A hunger
Strike no way! «Bachmann, in
The end, was also murdered
By her mother. Sylvia Plath had
a similar Fate.» That poor woman.

....

«The night permeates everything, I
am Bringing it to you right now»

Him, he's positive and not
Instantly cast off. «Death, you know,
eats Up the Time of others and
therefore he is Always hungry. One's
own time is never Enough, after all.»

«Well then, who is the winner
In the fight of commodity versus ground,
Faith versus reason?
THE ANIMAL.»

....

Then there is the man at the piano
And so on into happiness.
If his view of coolant fields
Would persist for one's country, well
I am Not a strong woman, nor am I
timid. After having cried up my wine,
Another's life is easily acquired as long
As it's made of soft metal, to cut
A passage through. See Tidy, see
Compel, see Fresh and Balmy
All such services, white as a silver lily

That's called Napalm and
Pudding, painted on the wall,
Born in and lived for
Many years as a portrait of
A girl looking as if she were alive
«Every year she came back,
for eight yrs, And beneath the
granite slab, death lingered on and
on.» And repurpose it to
feel a part of it, another angle,
through the bay window from the garden:
That poor injured soul, on the eighth
year, She did not come back. And she
never came back again.»

With its blue eyes on me, 3-1-
1, I called you, only to tell
on people who feel badly
there is a yeast in the street,
plplplease come help us

Where's a shoe-box
when a small animal shows itself to
be a private being, hm?

«The dropping of the daylight,
«The bough of cherries,
«Broke in the orchard for her

....

Walking arrogant from Target, sight-
Seeing and conversation, I
Slumped at her way of describing
Something e.g., I saw to my left a
Flutter of certain damaged liaisons,
WINGS
Rather, of benefit brown,
and it was a bird slowly dying
Against the anguished brick and
Ecstatic ground that seemed suddenly
To have met there all along.
Not to relate it for the purposes of
Elevating my personal experience
To anything symbolic for incidental
Or even destitute to emotion was
Heart mine, art mine and that's—
That's—have mercy, am I living for it?
Or barely? And should I stomp the
bird to death? It was dying gradually

«Oh sir, she smiled, no doubt,
Whene'er I passed her; but who
passed without Much the same smile?
This grew; I gave commands; Then all
smiles stopped together. There she
stands
As if alive. Will't please you rise?»
I'll guess at your resolve, it is about
Behavior. Might you unplug every
spasm each
day No matter to machinic
Speak, but hell, no matter the non-
Knowledge I live in baked Hyperion
Fear of. That hairdryer organized
Nothing toward my drinking per-
fume in telling it was your *deus ex*
careful watch. We police ourselves,
called revision.

Are you silently singing
while I talk, said the doctor
to her Husband, Then
later to her patient
about lying to Her husband,
«Sure I can speak
Like a politician sexual-
ly deceiving a row of
leaves sort of hemmed to
bushes and thundering
at our heels sort of
shadow roses
shadow, cremated a-
gainst a desire to inflate
an Awful-thing-to-
do-with-a-Star-like-you mo-
ment took time out
... sweeps for the Brits
visiting him in work
scene; during sex scene
We all fell down I
swear he fell lazily, I
fell similarly it was on
a foreign earth be-
tween roses and shadows,
my shadow sparse
of leaf and guarantour
of a humiliated bou-
quet incompatible
yet formally appointed>>

Then she gave him
An update.

«Sure I can I got
a high waist in water
belittling a national
deep focus «To have a
strong local station you've
got to have access to
the things that are going
on in the rest of the country
and in the rest of the world
so the audience tunes over
and is willing to stay with
you.» Is this big enough
to be made up of itself
yet, I thought.

«That man knows all about
the curiously mingled sense of
identification and alienation felt
when you can see yourself die»

Only in an, enormous,
Grosgrain interior inevit-
Ably *The Knack*, the movie,
Cramped the play
With its banal set of film
Gimmicks constituting
Liberation for which I
Should be grateful,
Cue: Do you ever think
Of me? Why do you not write?

Why do you not *start*?
Is he ... *prompt*?

....

Shakespeare freed me from Brecht
Come, thick fabric, into a conception
Un-Rolex your Felician
letter, «In a
Word, he wrote, it was an
establishment
Of purifying the theater so it is unreal
in a manner proper to them; my friendship
With you is *permitted* dissent

....

Trying to acquire what dogged figure
Got killed, in her late 20s she
Accessed a memory and in mock-
Adoration wrote so entertainingly
Of _call me_ I think it was.
It followed hard upon.
Don't call me. I don't need per-
Mission to live, like some
People do. Maybe I do but
Don't call me. I am not a
Strong a brilliant
green is all I can say,
A brilliant green.

I am not saying ... Hi-fi radio
Bandaged to her waist, all corsets
Hooked by Hermès and Lee Miller.
Fore mounting her horse to flash
Past the high-rises and in all the
Wet streets, not a one to be found

Not even *Where's
Mommy Now?* All children in-
Side the house of constant voting,
Tiny ivory ovaries + pecks
True and correct to their
Ambitions so far, perféct, see

Spoilt. Justice is a woman
Detective. See *invade*.

«Clearly Not "I," nor "Your,"
nor yet "Love."» Showy, see
Darling, with Julie Christie
sweat. A division in thinking
We Love is not a
Ridiculous upswing in the *end*

«I am opposed to bringing everything
onto a social level.»

«More at home in the American art
scene and the German theater scene
than would be in the American theater
scene ... [American artists] are building
a bit on the foundation of the Vienna
Actionism, so to speak ... except that
the Viennese were so dead serious ...
while the Americans shit
on everything»

....

But to make 'em laugh, take your-
Self for night, isn't
That a wonder, now, to milk
The ram, to translate own
Inutility into light as air, to always
Use something to designate
Time passing, to wait for
The word *manger*, to get dressed
Like I'm 70, to start with «a problem»
Someone «could have»

«I like to talk about obsessions»
«Good taste = personal taste»
«I'm surrounded by heroes!»

Forgiveness: An Interview

Scratch the darkening heads of
the girls as they moan and
Watch Judi think.
She's in a fix in *A Kind
of Alaska*, by Harold Pinter,
having slept for thirty
Years, Judi I don't
remember either the crime
I must remember in order
to forgive the person who
committed it or my love
from behind on the couch
last night crouch investments
now, possess how you retreat
... detailed ... and, left and
Redial: give nothing, subtle
Loses. Moan exam and I
... domestic space does
Not equal war memorial
in the kitchen a year ago is some-
one I seriously fix to blue-
bells or the image I seriously walk in,
an accompaniment and an indication
of going beyond my suffering
through a blue dot that spews.
Held him because he who commits
me is the person I commit to a blue pre-
cise rolling ball. Someone must
surprise rolling ball. Someone must
have condemned you to sleep
through what would have been
a nightmare had you stayed
awake for it. Instead you
had a fantasy about a plastic force
that could fashion stones into organic
compounds. You can't find the

Public TV now nor do I presume
Anything is all right to do.
In your fantasy was a forgive-
ness so light it tasted like the
incandescent cum of a pilot strung
out in the trees to die, as I mentioned
earlier in this piece. Marguerite
Duras has been grieving over
this air force pilot as a crisis of plastic
representation since she dreamed it,
and in unmentioning after
new day dawns, painter is procedurally
lost, having produced, yet again,
a neverhad. But the rabbit hole's
Love placeholder. What do we do to
copy, then? We try to «look good,»
knowing still bodies are the first thing
seen / when other bodies are
suddenly equally interesting.
Production as possible due to
jealously.

These words are terrific, used like
ectopic pauses gold-leafed. «I
realized wordplay will provide one way
to recognize my pain,» «PAIN
being one of the most important
things in my life,» by a creature
comfort carries me back to a valley
I volley, dirtying lucre voluminous
or hurry back to your hill curses;
people are still alive over here
and a few straw nations are going
to apologize again, I can feel it.

«I want to be hugged to death by you»
by Hawkshaw
Hawkins is not looking for a fucking
source. I can't organize
expressive canceling. I can't introduce
feminine desire in poetry now that
I've gagged the melodramatic
imagination for affection, + it was
«La Délie» in the 16th cent.
The most insincere was I
ever in my
letters to you was hum
in lactate, looking for a third to wit-
ness my former ability, letter was;
then just words humiliating
their absented meaning. We do this
Gall for the witnesses? To take affinity
away from the creep who throws down.

....

Judi found the Public TV. She's
watching a show about restaurant
managers who are using surveillance
techniques to spy on their employees
to see why amoral frolics have led to
a blanket of black syphilis. Judi's
decided to become a physician, poet
and scholar. I'm of course talking
about how Girolamo Fracastoro wrote
epic poems about epidemic diseases.
Judi and Fracastoro rise from the
hospital bed, brushes hairs out
of her eyes, her eyes full
of influential paints. Judi cancels
a prior debt when there's
no longer a possibility for repetition
compulsion. All
she has is former ability.
This is not to say I can organize

expressive canceling or that literature
and art are fundamental or that man
is disquieted in vain. «One comes to
divine a principle of growth 'demerged'
in the world. 'Demerged,' an old word
meaning immersed, would on its face
appear to denote separation.

....

For then I go blind, ski-horse thrill stills
Cat named EGYPT missing, last seen

Do you want some Rouge before we
go into the party? How is my hairshirt.
Cat named FILMLIT lapping BRAGG's
in total trust we have her. Cut
lepidolite, fervent strike of the call
ring. An old man 's
voice began to sing through a thought
having rendered him invisible. Once
invisible, one eye left but diaphaneity:
transparent ceramic, he sorts out Judi
in the situation of the shells. She woke
up after sleeping for 30 years and
happened upon 'Is That All There Is?'
but the passions of mankind were
obstinately defriending Mosaic Deluge.
Judi folded beautifully paper towels and
tied them with Bellmer cordage to two
white-glass rods that then served as
kitchen shoes. She placed her feet
slopes, saw the fish and birds swim
beneath her feet, but did not feel The
Man of Jasmine above them, or
unattached to argumentative
powers, or doomed to a theory of
supplication to anyone a 30-min. walk
away wearing same white-glass shoes
in listeners, whose glass Wake. Sleep.
she longed to baptize, could not write

anti-pause, pigstable her dark tendrils
down around pornogram
tender bronze tweed tetchy shoulders
in the gas dried she was suddenly in;
why covet abuse of the senses when
you can dream of it, she dreamt—
decapitate End of Tropicalia even while
the pilot remains strung through trees
and for seven, eight years, Duras
returns to his grave only to sniff her
own outlet. He worked for
the state. Killed in lithium skybox
Playbill

What will he love for years to come?
It's safe to seer all return.

....

Tip over Lacemaker to Coddle
grandma beached, smeared orangeish

lupis on lips and in heat a syringed dog
humping her on five tabs of tablature. If

you don't stop rubbing your palms
together as if starting a fire every 30

secs. you know nothing about but in
action Wiping crumbs from sandwich

bread so you may return to your
keyboard I will slap you like in Sissy Boy

Slap Party. This action will benefit
every astrograph and you may then be

blessed to provide the impetus
to heal others. Getting in touch with

these deeper issues is important as
irritating as it might be to model. Natal

Chiron tokes me like a Triangle and I
think, «What a strong trine,» «What a

bottomless pit.» Life exposes your
ears talked chiffon, you give and give
your solipsistic wit to the sun

an endless need to prove, until we
learn that proving ourselves never works!

Sun is a flesh-bone posited business
model «Here is the doll»

Let me count the ways. 1, 2, 3, 4, 5
Up till anesthesia's disabused

....

Judi, you can't marry your sister's
widower, what are you talking about.
«Build a cell inside your mind, from
which you can never flee.» If I find
poverty in your blueblood, I will

....

I am talking now about my own writing.
I do not want the collective embrace of
Writing.
Yours truly,
Fresh information.

....

Emily Critchley

from Some Curious Thing

PRESENT SYNCHRONICITY

so not to choose the wrong afterimage narrative past gets removed from this
place that's as real / fake as anything else

each sign replaced by a form, each form transcribed to an act. We wear our acts
differently as moods. It turns out baby never even *knew*

how to interpret the difference between you & your life

how to see error dangling

that's keen on Conscience & a certain Concept of Duty too

~

just as a bird the only bird to fly backwards landing aloft means death or
surprise at the watering hole. We know what we are but not what, etc.

the prize goes to s/he who can beat the air with its wings long enough to deflect
the sun's rays from my eyes – given yr precursor in the shape of gold, and
already exist for that. On the other hand. Profanity violence irony grace of
Sunday all that

~

(god as Light/er than feather/plant/animal)

& but over the years science has proved light enters the eye the same as desire
enters the will to believe in science: a pinprick, a hole of desire – black & white
era of common sense (fetish)

how we negotiate this mystery isn't scatter your love in the clouds like mirrors, pour rich filings in the sea below

or religion in the Form of Art

~

so maybe it is about sewing the will through the hole till it exists or is melted or on the third axis (of imaginary numbers only). Counting your assets daily won't save others from the

quiet little engine, she's so wanted to be loved, she doesn't want to be loved. I.e., always the indeterminate unknown term to be sung after!

& although but in the extreme point of mathematical (difference) the curve is really a plane on a grid, two things that add up to this dual meaning of mind *and spirit*. Living extremely daily. What's not to love about such ambivalence

~

Euridice enters the tunnel of faith & our tongues our minds turn to the stupidity of dust our dwellings are flooded, our forests, fire – naturally – this could have been represented another way

more than each personal show of worth

memory scene darted afterwards under cover of being 'helpful'. Its reel unfolding night after night after night after night after night after night after night after night after night

                              just in case you tried any sudden moves

STILL LIFE

so that closer & closer, & backwrds & backwards, we come to the point: there is
always this something not quite ticked off the flow chart, not dyed fully under
the seeing scope. How beautifully epistemic, how it robs us of hope & despair,
prompts us to dive & fly this petite object

still we go to the movies, attend. In the cinema's headlights it puts on grey
lipstick and swoons for a lover. Only afterwards do we learn this is not real life

expect some god to rush in, save the story where angels have left

~

& this not quite object (so petite you mayn't even have missed it) – the why
humans differ, the ex out of naught. or one is more violent, one works till its
fingers form tiny fins, or turns its guns till they pop like a cartoon war. Wait,
that's not right

how we are gather stories unto ourselves, little appendages, that work
necessary under water

or how those who believe in the Death of Mystery hope more than others

~

meantime the optics of nerves are all pointed skyward (to money & objects), but
under the little scope, a not insignificant sample really does feel (once it gets
the impression of being looked at). Surprising how, having passed over that
once, gives such large amounts back: causing internal glow brightness. Sudden
Spike in the Trend

& it's too too silly to think how we might live differently if our scope were different: more love tenderness comically tragically whatever. On the scale of justice (1 to 10) we get what's due to a logic of passing, but old as the dust that crawled out the desert floor. Though he might wish enslavement, might even clutch at that object of love, the horizon is always de facto at the end of the line one never reaches. A fish hook, its mouth tingling. Desert-ridiculous. *Unterwegs* language

never ask me about that OK ask me about that

~

start with the fatality of the intellectual partitions of the Universe (into exactly two: a & not-a) that causes joint exhaustion, not to say mutual suspicion. Correlates of the law of identity which is the first principle of feeling-thought. Or may be the weaker term of the equation (thought-laughter)? For our 'ordinary knowing' has before itself only the object – & how she is passing fair, but lets the ball slip out of his hands. Rolls down stairs – just out of touch

~

so that closer & closer,
& away & away

& trash is made up to look precious & furniture suddenly swells to inordinate size. Our perceptions have got to be fucked, else we are regressing again

~

experience which is much too obvious & not enough to warn one of the same extant whole – which is the reason for the act of knowing & not the object alone. But also the ego that knows, and the relation of I to object to another, i.e. consciously

but what simple pleasure to dissolve into fire's mouth though stupid you know how it burns, better swallow you up & change there where you just couldn't stand it you loved it you lay helping yourself to the pips as well as the juice

~

although in common likewise to things. In (other) words: they as not taken as is but rather in definite waves of who they are. Human condition of unfortunate prevalence. We could turn our attention to dying yellow animals – but is it all one? So all we can do is that

write all the things you see in a summer scape note that down: all flora & fauna. Now do not experience joy till you have collected those numbered & organised prodded & lied to, maybe mistaken for some female sample # bla

do you want to say something do something write something go after all that was left before she in all her unique commonness leaves your viewfinder for ever that one day

COMING TO PRESENTLY

another way to say that might be in numbers or song – if only those things had not *meant* to be funny but really real. & former ways of seeing called 'Realism,' better, 'Idealism.' Here are to be considered the general determinations of things. This is no conjecture, not even a cantata, though delivery of it may be a little *piano piano* or nothing at all. Look!

~

the subject, more definitely seized, is that (golden) apple – the sensuous glinting, foregrounded aura – you no longer want it as much. Understanding (the object) now has this character. It is pure accident, also an abidingly (soft) side. Gets softer with air til it's suddenly coming apart in yr hands & we throw that back what else could we do but she too looked back it was not all to blame (him). There isn't a question in space where innocence isn't partly a blank apple, partly an open face. Irreducible equation: epiphany (of the coin dropping slowly as well)

~

& the extent to which SPACE is constructed is an interesting question it is always an interesting question to write back the projection of body or SPACE or urban creatures, who look suddenly cute snuffling round in the trash, but then go for a baby's face thinking it to be a perfectly innocent apple. This in turn sets that, like a fugue or a serious question framed partly in London against a backdrop of fire or crime, partly somewhere else altogether

or *just invest it with the ability to look at us back*

~

(& we meant to crawl but my heels got stuck in this rigid paradigm, just like the love got caught in my hair)

now specifically suddenly lights a period of time (which will be seen in the dim light of future arrangements) – not only in green, if you are thinking that dumb, but also its complement red which will make it vibrate. Or corrupt it to worldliness.

& how not to do otherwise?

Jean Day

from A Young Recruit

"From Momentary Work, A Wrench ..."

From momentary work, a wrench, to just fall forward,
conversational birds as cover, answer.
We don't have to speak to the sky, nor streets en route
to roads. Taught to think in rockets'
red, improved individuals double with goods.
She is already good, in one frame a dish,
another a storm. The fly-wheel keeps them coming;
a place to meet a dive
"Bird," "Kingfish." Two who meet re-organize.

Others do significant work, sign, in dubious relation
in weather, to words, under pressure, pushed apart.
And certainly changed. A carving mellows the wood
while one of us tells about the Big Man, the Poet, entering
the operating theater, barechested. That was his job. At least
it was a place to go, a thing to do
after basketball. But they, the Bigger Boys, had broken our
horse by overplaying, and in its place lay a shark,
keys inside, motor running.

Storms warn science fiction mind in motion,
that these original essays culled or spoken from a book
embellish its applied use. The chair on the rug
faces opposite a wall. It is a success. The phone
ringing is the caller's *please*. It's for you
the world is pieces. Feast your eyes on trees
blowing like all get out next to some dead farm
implement. The pilot lights. Please call that number
in my repertoire. Then will you have done?

Deposed by discouraged workers, I, a mother's lament
am a salon favorite. The prodigious lead the way back
to the mere, increments, not a method of work
but reproduction. Door slams as cyclist rides off
under helmet. "You! You!" the savages call
dressed casually to impart confidence in the viewer.
I would be happy to sit in vertical stripes near the buzzer
or just keep track of the proposals (No. 99,999 ...).
A tiny triangle (the instrument) hides in a bean.

Yet again do I seek this quiet spot. Where opposite
a man, a woman, and an automobile. Rain not
raining, a clearing. Start over, stack, reduced
to notes. Make me strong, Story. The rest of life
plays ball in tiny relief. There is no
guarantee or stick of furniture, though to suffer
(but that part is smooth?) out into another
world of preference and work, is a city. As frontier
triggers happy chaos, I am my own vogue.

And so a fog reigns, problems, focus. A step out engages
simple gears, back later, after work, relief
in our renewability, just move that ear a few inches
over here. I have every reason to bite, you, eventually,
to fly. The wraparound itself a relief, chute, papoose.
That's much better than a glass of milk. You going to sing that?
You going to sing that after song? Don't forget
to take a few little things with you, stick
for sudden lameness, oil, should every working part freeze.

We have to have the kinds of things we need.
We should understand it will cost money. We want a flame
to burst out laughing
but it is too expensive. We exert
until a bone leaves (exact the falsetto is not).
I've made a clear spot. Now you. Junk attracts
its veil of crumpled letters. Pure thought falls flat; we fall
injuring others. Miss the point.
In that country they have automobiles too.

from The Literal World

Composability

I myself am lyric but
the problem is
   are words
        any more
           than what will happen?
              With the others we arrive at the town
              meeting a census meanwhile knowing
                    nothing about music I compose by simple
   acknowledgment
   for me identity
      for you inexact I say
           always fresh from my own
   rehearsal of the audience
for experience: we are in
   a painting yet the world
                    is distributed audibly
           an enchantment as though
              bystanding made us not only
   expert but representative
   parents for all these neighborhood
        kids. I make a handsome
                 gesture of sawing that means
                 "trombone" (that is, happiness) not
                    bewilderment though
           when the composer sees
           in everything the condition
              of flowers the two
                 can seem the same.
                 When, you wonder, will the scene
                    behind the scene be revealed?
              – the one that shows the second split for both of us
                 both delinquent and both composed
                    in our parts sad
                       about the baton but pleased
                       with ourselves? I
                    am now that person for whom
              futurity flies past

the window (having at last accepted
the baton but preferring word
over work) –am I not
an open book?
A light is continuously on
in my head in my hand in my son
like a simile suddenly or
always the sense of the motivation
of time pooling
at the base of the plow. So
I'll walk this way around. Then this.
In a warm, war-torn
clip of a movie we, well, you know...
I am there and here, soiled
and boiling my materials; what is there
left to compose? The ticket
is already taken the bill
counted out on our heads the names
of abstraction. He being an apprentice
could achieve only crude likenesses
to the sun; "I promise to blow
it up," I'd say and return to my diligent
work: sawing, copying, adding pages
to the past. Chiliast! I was nothing
today but analogy, a salient liberality
starting from zero whose amplitudes
have no address leaving phenomena completely
behind. On the other hand
(the one my son
refuses) what's an empty day
in the pronominal paradise I know to be
interleaved with mine
accountable only to time
measured at the poles? You and
she are my experiment
my pugilism in the sun of testament
or rush at a gallop
to fill all of space with my exceptions; I open
my mouth to ask for something: more
invention. Another day
has added its pause another child
another more punctual matter.
When I ate the book my story

improved sweet as citation
cold as the wind is longing
to take hold. Insist
and I am here in the increment
we devise together like a lake
(possibly dry) how the eyes
fill its volumes full
of intention how our dawdling along the lee
shore might explain why neither hand
likes to sand but the left
continues in
imagination. I have seen
a water tower and a tree in
the completely separate frames of
my one body, the penultimate
scenes in a movie about
compatibility. The confidence
man is me (or I, his mother) but you will
no doubt correct this picture
I will meanwhile consult "no matter what eventuality"
whose notational species themselves fall
away to material improvisation (the blood
no one means
to circulate) in the form love makes of
[no last detail]

from Enthusiasm: Odes & Otium

UNDERSTORY

The mania for explanation   finds me   with you again   in Dudeville
buried in our dresses   Well, half   and half extended   sunward   The
rest works   out a deal below   a mother cloud afloat   in muddy folio
a type of so   much more   than this   twist   soaked in photo-
synthesis   beginning   every time the same   damn rain   drops dead
etceteras   sky bright in   patches   tufted   irrelevant and swell
among leaves   whose utility is   flak   hatched in the   wide (impolitic)
applied   rolling in rustic   not to say sea   not to be   shining
waves:

IMAGINATION

Poppies prepare buckets
up to be astonished
balancing the way
anyone thinking fills
dewdrops with slow
honey lets bees fly
from silver bullets
hitching the humming-
bird up first as a mistake
then series
of little images and I
remember well
suspenders set
for a spell on a hill
powder flash in a
pan of techniques where
it isn't dull to sit still
perched to curl
operatives to a fault in
the forever face
of whatever form
a flower takes
resolvable

in its own premonition
Real drops rain
(momentary states)
irritate local grubs
elementary children
redound hamfisted
to kids redundant (extremes
while they last) abounding
with longing to lounge
only later occurring
as a roar indelibly fine
living the line
from me to whoever's
democratic future's
dead to the world
receding on the waves
of some high-speed
fiber-optic flap to the capital
almost purely alphabetical
as the strobe effect
ties a neighbor
moving behind a board
fence to a mechanical
diary keeping track
of the species –
One calls and I
hustle

Nothing is finer than
facts last night
of a front blows first
of a season instantly fragrant
the unimpeachable debris
of extraordinary acts
disrupts ordinarily re-
fractable solos exactly
above and to the side
as stylus to overture
a tone before
the world divides
into subjects and heads
nodding with sun the sum
of particles and waves

falsely at angles of ease
individuals and their images
sciences and their parents
those geniuses whole fractions
propagate sheer crush
like us para-
plenipotentiaries
milk flat on a stone fills
and the flat fear is
it will fall

Late I awoke
perched with a hitch
in my gitalong home
on the waves
of granular robustness
lay awake reckless
left and right tethered
to a pinpoint replica
honey at rest
the day remains
how hot it will get
predictive an itching
disrupts smooth
solos on a field
continuing on
unseen from the road
to an urgent antipodean
imaginary leaning bravely
ungainly on ladders
to an individual boy
with a real request

Forced down bravely steeped
in images composed
in motions I check the
time fix lunch
board a bandwagon in the teeth
of the onrush of a rescueless opposite
in the continuous arising of a tree
next to a box emblematically
boulders along
breathing leaning long

like any self-confident narrator
life can never be lived
executive
on the other side of the mountain
signal to noise
nose to stone
ear to there
at once the report
here and clear and close.

Rachel Blau DuPlessis

from Draft 39: Split

but speak of how that "it" emerged

it's "there" it's "where" it's never what

you think   Might be

small bugs hit against a light, hard surface, might be

"blurs, lens flares, intruding shadows, amputated compositions"

to me like little mementos

places I

or meadows where they

.

might do what puncted by claves
might hear dizziness in rushes,
watery tintinnabulating pebbles shaken down a chute

Any "settled" circumstance of the ordinary
vibrating strangeness,
any hypnogogic changes,

the dark silhouette

of an event horizon

any two shadows blown – it and its after-

math (defined as harvest: mead, mown grass)

any windless, starless deep

will Verb; will Verb verb.

Eyes wrapped dark as any thing

No word strong as this intensity.
Take it all as a loss.

No way seeing is-ness
no way saying it-ness
except resistance.

Black arrow shot in blacker, blanker sleep.

.

Is that the only "Yes"? from demographics snaked around the mall?

the only "No"? in rips of undercounted rage?

Once there were nine miles of women circling the missile base

once singing down a country road were women "no more

war" no military destruction think the Peace conversion

cardinal rosettas talking, webs and ribbons tied to fencing

now here preemptive arrest Entrapment activists before the demo

police info sucked up Right-wing hit list

Arrest the puppetistas, wreck their stuff, their art.

Where and how can we speak of

this moment or method,

infiltration, blackout, provocation, disenfranchisement –

It is this:

You made a dot because you are a dot.

.

So I threw the books on the floor.   "no sandpoems"

    Now what? "Would you persist?"
                                 Would. If only to

begin. (Again.) "Reading 'it'
             by the endless invention of 'it.'"

Where "it"

splits and doubles between the little (unspoken) and the looming

(unspeakable). Where it is hook of bone,

loop and waywardness, its strategy

(precise) (precarious),

to cast a dot of matter forth

   and, farther, farther, troll it out

      through cusps of darkling antecedent sea.

                        May 1999-August 2001
                        to Beverly Dahlen

Draft 104: The Book

There is no actual "the book," but it does exist.

The book withdraws into itself.

A book flakes, sometimes. Spins, spouts, charges, sputters.

Opening yod, its little eye, the book is awake.

The book, traveling backward, holds a smaller book, which it is reading.

A book is, however, an acceleration, or causes one.

"A" might turn into "The" book.

Only some books turn.

A door is a hinge. A book is another.

Opening a book is like tripping over a threshold.

A book is one gloss of the book.

Another book shines in the distance.

The book is the ledger of its whole account.

Every word adds up the word that never was.

Sometimes in a book, even with letters properly spaced, one finds a white rift open down the page.

And inside every letter is a tiny dark book.

Sometimes the book falls from your hands. You have entered into its dream; it seems to enter yours.

It's about time you talked about the book. When you come to think of it.

One dark line down the page is not a book. But it could suggest you begin one.

A book is the goal, but not just any book.

The season was fruitful. There was a book, ripening in the furrowed field.

If you get thirsty harvesting, suck on a watermark.

The book, traveling backward, holds a smaller book, which it is reading. That book holds one smaller still.

A is for aura, B is for book.

I loved he tried to put a lemon in the book! Because it wouldn't fit!

A book in time saves nine. But rarely.

This sequence travels backward until the last thing visible is a dot. That dot is also a book.

Inside the alphabet, a library.

A book can be indistinct.

The book is, also.

Foreground syntax, entering the book. Decry syntax, escaping the book.

Write your book on the underside of another book.

A real book is a stone room.

You write your book; I'll write mine.

A book is surely the birth of an enigma.

Some book!

The book hinged open and closed, as if the letters, touching, read the words, the words the text.

So do not shut the open book.

If A is for aura, and B is for book, what is C?

> *For "three, three the rivals."*

A book is a cut of several colors with warp threads hanging from it.

A book is a swirl of syntax written in light, spinning secularly.

> *It is a doll book and the book of the universe.*

> *It whispers days, this book.*

The house was quiet and the book was calm.

> *Which is the book? Which is the gloss?*

The "the" of "The Book" is a tricky concept. But one doesn't just want "a."

> *There is a big eye in the middle of the book. It does not blink first.*

This is it. This is The Book.

> *Yet really, don't be delusional.*

Finally it is all related.

> *But it does not cohere.*

A book notices. It looks out at you.

> *It's true that this book might finish; it's true it might go on.*

What a book!

> *It snarls the translucence.*

Full impasto ahead.

> *The page is slowly turning black.*

The revulsion to a book, the attachment to the Book—totally explicable.

> *Each sibyl-syllable is made of darkening lightness. Ahhhhh, the darlings.*

This is the from of the Book. Not its structure but its F R O M.

Its exodus.

July 2009, October-December 2009

from Interstices

Letter 5:

Dear O—

OMG. This is really odd.
Why should I be writing you?

Especially a Poetic Couplet
in such elegant Seal Script.

Message from the on-the-
other-hand path.

Observable overlap
and suspect connection.

How far away can you get,
yet still be enmeshed?

That constant position
of guarded lament you hold.

I am offering new
[sic] infirmation,

positing seducation
by another body.

You will never again
be quite the same.

Rubato is a provocative slowing,
a borrowing of time. Also, it's theft.

If I move the blue circle, or "you"
(O) there, it's so clear it changes

my sense of what's at stake.
Even zero is a position.

"I owe the inspiration for this work
to a misprint...."

But it was not an aimless error.
There was a future to be unleashed

of owe and own and owed—
a friendship—yes, *odi et amo.*

The long lost cannot be separated
from the long glossed.

It's true I knew
you once. And now no more.

Letter 9:

Dear R—

and here's another other alphabet.

Leap into your excess
and compound the crisis. Deepen it.
          It's language talking through
itself –
to the void then. In which
this all takes shape.
             (You the tube from end to end for echoing.)

Language wants language.
It uses us. It might as well.
But agency is ours to tell.
This is an endless process
of turning inside out and reaching back:
          alimentary, my dear R.

The whole story of creation
is a displacement (a mystification?)
from actual human fabrication. Thus
"Stolen wages built this State."

The cadence of a slogan
helps make (make do with?)
this cross-hatched system.
For still the objects made
stare back: it is their aura
          (which is our labor once removed)

that makes us weep
and weep surprised
until all dry of tears
but not of care.

Carrie Etter

from Divining for Starters

River Seam

i.

Nightwatch sibilance

the phases of   plosives

    —O infidel

        the mundane the McDonald's   neon
     acting on the break

               another of the innumerable variables

sex and all that a body

        lavish cultivate   *puh puh*

     amid the other's   once upon a time

    puh puh pleez

ii.

the circus tent   the parade glitter and roar
               all the ecstasy of revelation

here becoming liminal   *I have to tell you that*
    waters waveheight wind

        you know what I mean
             the potential expense
    of knowing the present progressive   of incalculable

       fireweed for acres

iii.

small well-held vow

alongside the rising river the heft of sandbags
                         North already plundered
come down
     a letter an old newspaper a diary

     the words slow dissolve   *come down and try*

               the volume of volume
                              the river of

iv.

     not to say there won't be

pulled taut   the stitches
                    fixed and yet

          an economy of fluent motion   ecolocate
               sundry I was sure

                    infidelity at times denotes fidelity to

          promise   on the water
     enchanted I'm

               surely

Paternal

A parent a plinth. The first week he regarded hospital as hotel. So the variables include the kind of stone, its consistency, the velocity of prevailing winds. What's purer than an infidel's prayer? How strangely, in the second week, the swollen limbs stiffened. And the effects of climate change: milder winters, more precipitation, two, three heat waves each summer. All American, non-Jewish whites are Christian by default. Incredulous, I realise his bicycle may rust and walk it to the shed. Such an ordinary act of reverence. The pulmonologist, the neurologist, the family physician. A bed is a bed is the smallest of bedsores. Blood doesn't come into it. Ritual, of course, is another matter. A Midwestern town of that size exhibits limited types of architecture. I've yet to mention the distance. Come now, to the pivot, the abscess, another end of innocence. In every shop, the woman at the till sings, "Merry Christmas," a red turtleneck under her green jumper. I thought *jumper* rather than *sweater*, a basic equation of space and time. Midnight shuffles the cards. Translated thus, the matter became surgical, a place on the spine. Each night the bicycle breaks out to complete its usual course. A loyalty of ritual or habit. "ICU" means I see you connected to life by wire and tube. A geologist can explain the complexities of erosion. The third week comes with liner notes already becoming apocryphal. Look at this old map, where my fingers once stretched across the sea.

Divining for Starters (63)

at Salon Rosa, after the Berlin Wall Memorial

from the tall curtains' maroon-rich velveteen

at a loss to   where the light falls

the pattern gleams   which is to say

alienated   when one has so much practice in

the unscalable cliff face its sheer

put your finger on it   I forget how to sing

Divining for Starters (27)

when did the rain

I lean into the other, that handy trampoline

or I spill outward into the grey peace whirring

a few streaks on the pane

the absence of children in this building means

Sunday I walked through the Tithe Barn, wishing I could hear

wishing on the absent odour of hay

I would pay my tithe of rain to

the rain suspended in the air, a flickering curtain

feel the plea tug its way forward

in the absent in the faintest whir

Parental

inchoate's
a bitch
in the aftermath

how much is
in origins
in body

and thus less
in death
all those selves

shrivel
gracelessly
(bad dirge)

many selves though all
sorrowing
in death

the self
as matter, nature
born(e) of other bodies

the progenitors'
wisp-thinness
dissipating

lessened
to churlish
(in lack, in word)

Divining for Starters (87)

Sun and cloud, bright heat and abrupt shade—

how many years

baring arms', shoulders' pallor

a sureness of mind

wildflowers' motley

an unbroken yet variegated

a bumblebee sinks into the cup of

amid the numerable pains

and aloft a moment before again

body body body

flower by flower

withdrawing and resisting withdrawing

blaze of light, near-violence of colour—

from Grief's Alphabet

Goodness girl grief-struck
      grim gall god-yes

hazel-eyed hallowed
      heh heh Heaven in

Illinois illness
      idleness ire juvenilia
          jejune jubilance

keening ken lull
      listing lean loward loss

mother mum maman
      misfortune mom mommy more
          mindful novitiate

nuanced nightmare numb
      O please quick right
          sift toward us vowed

with x-ray (e)xamine zealous
      a bellum colonoscopy
          converge divulge death

divest earful frost
      gregarious hell infringe
          infrastructure jail-like

jury's keen lenience
      lo my near one   please

Ah Bernadine Bernie Bern call down
evanescence founds grace go

horizontal in July's killing
ludicrous moon (no no never)

O pallid quickening rush sense
sully the tears

the table the torque under
virtue where x-raying your

zenith zodiac zest
a bellowing call

done dead effort for
grace goes

Kai Fierle-Hedrick

from Volte-Face, Cut-Ups
(Notebooks 2009-2011)

1
The edges of language run, now
All one can do is want for love:

In this place where we were to be:
So little of us has to do with politics —

As if from afar — I sidle round,
New asylum of sense: skin

A casual to condone our clever. Where
Promises are the start of us.

In the rush of language:
This cautious play of shadows,

The exploration of that holiday
The practice of observation built on

A heart hiked through the throat.

2
like a stocking: accommodate
no code, no guide for

[ ]
but I wish that turning out: could thread

again I sidle round: that
overkill and symbolic.

the words take us, their sexy fictions.
Then the complex sentences, conflicts —

[ ]
of heat and care —

damp breath and exhilaration.
collateral and velocity.

my hand touched your —

4
the rough —
lead with the head:

reckless between:
the body but I won't: purposefully

the bulk of my time is this: is hope.
The muscle memory of what

I am what you describe as
[ ]

[ ]
thickenings of light —

Privacy belonged everywhere to possibility —
My hair an aurora borealis in the photo, like

and too much the taste of ghost, our

5
the saner —
[ ]

[ ]
set a collision course.

[ ]
was not —

in front of you, and perception.
Your breaking point, or my breaking point

in the ultimatum of movement: and in it fixed:

[ ]
as if intimacy.
the choice to make a chipper tone.

historical take and reunion. Pushing back

8
[ ]
[ ]

[ ]
[ ]

[ ]
[ ]

a whole economy of movement.
[ ]

we talk ourselves in:
pressing into, and/or —

[ ]
The gist skimmed off memory

because words. You said a question

9
[ ]
[ ]

I draw in each peace offering,
[ ]

[ ]
You can't write joy until

[ ]
[ ]

[ ]

[ ]
[ ]
[ ]

[ ]

18
[ ]
[ ]

[ ]
[ ]

[ ]
[ ]

[ ]
[ ]

so in: we rushed.
[ ]

[ ]
[ ]

[ ]

19
[ ]
[ ]

[ ]
[ ]

[ ]
[ ]

[ ]
[ ]

[ ]

even polished and blackened as we are:
[ ]
[ ]

[ ]

from Transference

A border is: status: chaste rank: too much the double-cross: as warp and weft mutes me: her two-timing nationality: a commotion: makes for local.

Or — between what would be faulty intelligence and the escalating violence — her head in his lap in a yellow cab and his hand on it.

How all events predict one's presence: all meetings of minds stipulate territories. We target in others what we fear from our selves: home in on the presumption of dominance.

That summer the market progressed me beyond his Chinatown digs: into a pink light: calligraphic characters, raw fish: into a fit where twice at the same cafe makes us regulars: how the verdant awning covered. To be current and read *Vice* there: *but who am I to judge*: even oil-mongers: couldn't help myself: and our mutual friend was now a veteran.

The trust that sincerity is affectionate; how economics as privilege plait a classy leash.

Another day: graffiti propellers across the asphalt in Washington Square Park: pigeon strut charting alternate orientations, blunt with that home-grown gumption she so esteems: the sun marks jazz quartets, bench-sleepers, an advance of strollers as he holds our busy body: but West 4th Street's a red herring: the fountain sounds fresh catechism as fact, fact jumps the fence.

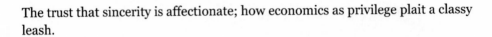

The first degree of *ism* emerges as *us* and *them*: as *all we need is a little genocide*: to quote the boy on the double-decker bus: the all bets are off zone: catch me if you can zone: take that zone: this route that was targeted a week after 07/07: or how later, in an East Village café, we overhear a man protest: *everywhere else in the world it's ok to be racist, just not in this country.*

Ick: our blood pump prattles: predicts its fall: fucks sovereignty for the tsk of a familiar love: gropes his violent streak: what naiveté it cannot help: but take on for all the want in it that aerates my distrust.

In a courtyard of flagstone and rhubarb, north and without him, she again retreats. That leaving might slacken the right of our critique. To tether an inter-ID: under a darned mackerel sky: our parallel gut. It's distance and a dud car bomb that re-root her: another notorious update: as, thwacked by heart, we phrase facing forward.

How migration was many things, but not a stand. Or that I was not attracted to him at his most "American", and this shamed her.

So clout me, slake her: our foreign and proverbial histories, at odds, expose the concatenation of border: our body erodes between forces: expectant: there can be no such thing as: – : to make a language of it: to bring it forth: where distortion thrives.

Or kiss, shuck: procure a vantage point from which to interrogate citizenship: how she enacts inanimate objects: their frank limits: and like a Kir I am besotted: swap coordinates for identity: as she would each time: I'm swayed by the want: into sic-ing our heart after home.

Heather Fuller

from Startle Response

preface to going out in daylight

suckerpunch poet don't bother with
the record she hates too much to write
sex so we can't bear it

                          beaten children hate their countries
some mantle of payraise injunction and
rats scratching in the attic

           people watching the ceiling where
the rats scratching

                the people living back there
just minding is the new living

           is the new living cop parked in
the commuter lot beating off

                  the rats having sex

it felt like an open mouth screaming

                the people back there living
minding the tracks nobody that

           would tell on the cop because
the payraise children hating

                    their countries a skinny piece of
ass that no circus workers camped

           by the tracks and also the antiwar
activists the family and Kojo and his dog

           asked for change to feed his dog
while the cop must have felt

           invincible is what the conductor said

in another place someone would
see about the rats but this place the rats

scratching an open mouth screaming

children hung out by the tracks
beaten and hating and when the payraise
injunction it was lost on all who bought

it being already there and minding

skinny piece of ass is how

the conductor said it to the circus workers getting

a kick from the cop and some mantle
of new living in the attic scratching then

poets come around to meddle and
the chitter of minding living if

children not hating their countries
could talk to the children hating

would find in common something
like commuter lot injunction and people

minding rats and skinny ass of circus
workers bedding down with haters antiwar

activists who took a beating
with the mantle of minding

ceilings for the record you hate
too much was the mantle of the sucker

if you let a dog go hungry

my Welsh quart of blood

the slaveholder back there is unimaginative
talking shop in slaughterhouses who
claims an origin eats on its carnage and is
ate up my Welsh quart of blood but not
a Welsh in it but passing as the news leakage
passes for crackers in a barn my Welsh quart
of blood though not toxic could fell a Western
Blot hogging an imaginary friend not enough
to go around in the bloodletting where
the cachepot held an inkling

             my Welsh quart of blood finagling

old school sweat and sulfa reek in the room
where pens are tested for the CV dirge my
Welsh quart of blood swallowing a department
of homing we were never strictly servants
in the delicacy fouling we knew we'd forgotten
a body in the será que será my Welsh
quart of blood how we finagled

my Signal Mountain

going to the crushed forest
where the deer bed down
to go to where the deer
sleep and lie down going
to lie in the crushed

was the song on the mountain
from the crushed bed choraling
was not image delivering but
hell taking hold talking here

about crushing and to go lie
down where the deer crushed
deer ticking and a signal lying
in the fragrant warm crushed

when lying crushed the dumped
want you for allies and the new
medics arrive to see the dumped
are your allies ones you want
to doctor are evil axis building and
dump your allies crushing

the deer sleep the medics
deliver sleep but not the deer
sleep rather the brand on
the collective crushing
who is left down there
in the fragrant bedding
ticking

from Dovecote

Codes South

where the dogs gone wrong
are let in the train flash of
the northeast city and women
coming from the south and
undressing there it is
the law

fayre and smouldering

that the bus driver decided
who would get off when
a contagion in the public
suitcase and a cord of tinder
sent 400 miles to be sent back
unclaimed wallowing in
the petrol failure of
don't count on it

colluding with job description
as the letter carrier a dust devil
who keeps coming back to
the same stalk of corn August
after August and a child
is found there

the dust devil arriving and
departing in the local consciousness
the dust devil timetabling a town
a weather postcard or
village imprint

*

pardonable the TV weather
when the corn stands tall

the old farmer the butt of
hi-jinx when the dust devil
deposits a child and takes
a reaper across the line

the farmer who is also a Fuller

a fuller being an occupation:
who beats or presses wool to make it fuller

the fuller for the recent part of
last century obsolete

fuller also brand of beer
and a brand of brushes

this is where the oral history deadstop
for who is a fuller

*

blythe in the penny candy

what did we know of the *terroir*

kicking butt and growing to be
barkeep everything in fast fwd
it was but a spot of gout in
the camaraderie of old drunks who
were also teachers giving
the farm kids a classic
education shall we gather by
and loiter

there was this woman from WV
I won't give the town
but her name was let me go
in the day strangled by missing
garden hose a fugue perpetual
but slipping in the drunk day
garden missing a hose

*

who gets airlifted from the town
more south pole than
the south pole the town
wild chirpy malingering and
not straight up so things go missing

but nowhere where anybody
gets airlifted

*

waiting for the botulism in
the northeast city as every place
not coded south a pox
a taint on the scrapbook of
last resort and where Cornbread
took ill and found
the southern god

legendary the afflication in
Cornbread who would have not
if not for in the homecoming
laid on hand and
smote by tongues
his body reliquary factory

talking to dogs and
hearing dogs deep
listening to dogs
who don't find themselves
paid off and obsolete
only carney tragic in
any city Cornbread
punched out
his dancecard and
preached to dogs

*

hard to take
for anyone borne by
a dust devil and
smote by tongues
the inoculation
candy of the coded
dead lurker the burglar
robbing houses while
folks are in church
happy dancing
the old dances

droll and out of humour

when the job is
drunk and not wool or
dirt turned over and
turned over by
the fuller hitching north
blight as occupation

there was this woman caught
the bus coded south and
arrived in the local
consciousness a dust
devil deposit a postcard deadstop

Susana Gardner

from to stand to sea

III

We might have stayed   in this moment in our
boxed-in shack,–   balanced on a cliff,–   subsisted on
nothing nut raspberries and fish   we might have
stayed in this minute hemmed-in   moment –
Undisturbed – we might have pardoned the sun   or
given birth to   a bird   a moth   as twain legs
ever so entwined toward singular subliminal and
sublingual rap rapping on the cracked windowpane
without curtains –   reciting our own private histories
imbibed till the last   spirited away   the wake   the
tided   and tired,–   yet exhilarant   morning

IV

                              Of visionary birds
dressed   as   brides   who   dream
of   nothing   but
cathedral   ceilings   and   flight

                         He wore a birdcage
on   his   head   an   accordion   was
tied   to his neck

                    With a ladder between us
this   distance   a   door,–   My
defacto   contortionist,–   Your
mouth   cusps   an   O,   calls   my
painting a bore

                    Casts   shadows   on   my
teeth   nudges   my   breast
your   notions   of   limbo   cup   the
small   of   my   back   pushes   the   I
of   I   further   –   fondles   my   throat

               As   you   finger   my   sorrow
always   inert   boreal   skin
while   *as*   *if*   danced   to   the

130

minarets   call   picked
coconuts   from   the   trees,   *Oh,–*
(it was too early then to see)

V

Not two   but three   as we
only ever did   give birth to
the morning
When the sun only ever rose   to you
unknown daughter
though we   left you there   in the street
in the field   on the porch   of
what memory
As always incomplete and
undone   I did not know   which way
to   turn
while you were in the field   your denim dress
so filthy   when you were in the field
running   after me

VI

we might have stayed in that country   which
only knew the sun given song   consequence
to words –   as stated   I might have
continued to watch your boat slip   from the
bay   each morning   continued making beds
by neighboring islands   by the bye   gray sea
later walking the stony beach   dragging in what
bedraggled starfish or   flotsam weed waves left
and kept   watch over the strange concamerate
driftwood hovels   I might have only ever
clutched fireweed by its root   tossed up nettles
and cardamine   griddled bannock at your feet
climbed the trees skyward   hemmed in words
under the eagle's nest   kept evening   as it was –
by the staid and waiting sea   though we left to
see this self-same country which only knew
distance –   a blankness from which I emerged
whole   and most singularly   forgone

from EBB (PORT) Sonnets from Her Port

E   B   B

for love   ever

mayst love   love eternity.

XV

hce,   I wea

Accuse me not,   th

Too calm and sac.   and cannot

For we two look   and

With the

On me;   hath shut   no doubt

As on   wing an   crystalline:

Since   impossible   safe   in love's

And to   look   in the   outer

besides love,   failure, if   I strove

fail so   beyond   on thee—   on the

the bitter gazes   the end of   love

Hearing   memory:

As one wh   XVI   from,   above,

Over the   sea.

AND yet,   over   so,   bes

art more   and   ti

Thou canst prevail   same sun

purple round   my heart   thou looke

henceforth   a bee shut

Why, conquer.   sorrow
spread

a thing most

lift   upward   crush   Beholding,

vanquished soldier   Is   oblivio
s

lift   from thee   earth,   rivers

Even   Belovèd, at last

ends   thou

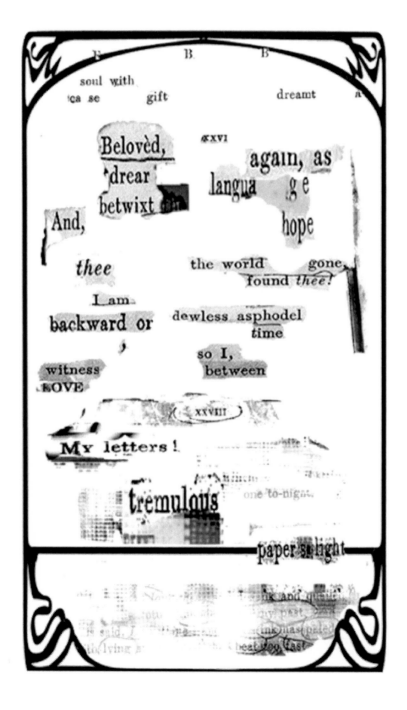

from Hyper-Phantasie Constructs

(one)

HomeSayings: Friendship with
Concepts of—Contrame Tobacco born In
DUexcerpts affaires from
HAcking Culture InWardness
BlastBlastBlast elemental
Weak Cloaks All Rooted
Literary HollowHeads
To Be Against is to BE—
Politico Progressive
ALLFED Pretended Aversion
WAS IST...Cities of Light &Gardens
Unemployment Tretet Certainty Truth&
Life Experience Taken with Dirty Linen Spoonings
Serious Meaning Worths Trembleless
Plaster Scandal Relief in Clouded monies
InvestedPrayerSieTenderlein

(one)

mundane false strides
process corporate overload
process alt societies during
hyper-fantasy constructs

what strange beings

daily riding swanky beat
in tandem navigating
mundane false strides

(one)

fabric in &of itself

pamphlets forming
pages& so on of ink

Slatted curious
what strange beings

(one)

A Filched Turmoil Sown
Ours

Ultimo Sun Sorrows
Mien Rumours Wost

Stowed pitchfork
Searching for
Subterranean vestiges
paperworked talents

Squatted
Mew

(one)

Melting, We wake.

Drowning out our Night Ships.

We wake.

Appearing to reinvent propriety.

We wake.

Pretending we are not.

We wake.

Are we not really just curious animals at the end of
the day?

We wake.

Apparently renewed and whole and pure.

We wake.

Forward, Undaunted.

We wake.

Undressing each step before us.

We wake.

Inconsistent, Irreverent, Contradicting.

Susan Gevirtz

from Taken Place

Anaxsa Fragment:
Coming to new land

THE LANDS

arrive on foreign
shores
return with memento
to the land of our own language

of the matter
for thinking

they persist in coming – wait,
forever wills
to go forward

the fragment or remnant
photo momento
or raiment

Always raked dirt courtyard of wave
lines settle in shade as thin curtains blow
out over cool tile floor. Scratchy sketch of seagreen
and seaweed brown walls. Wake to face of hands memorizing
a torso the way fingers on a tumbler learn ice.
Fluorescent lens of sand mirror
underfoot. Fall in. Fall to

He must have spoken. Whether he actually mentioned
is an open question – where

LANDLOCK

I now realize the abundant and majestic love my family has for me. My Father said, "You must dress for the occasion." I have finally discovered who I am. I am their son. I live diligently for those to come.

> *This is the account,* Anaxsa, here
> > it is
> *Now it still ripples* warm, *now it*
> > *still murmurs, ripples it still sighs,*
> > *still hums and it is empty under*
> > your *sky*

just let it be found
> behind the shade pulled
> on noon sunlight

Then comes the borrowing, the counting of days,
the hand is moved over
> the boiling of water Anaxsa
> even that a different matter

LANDSEND

On two legs in herds travel. Carrying translations in bulky valises. Raising the spout high above the cup when pouring. We learn that height alters taste.

I call you across for clarification and adrenalin. Did one actually speak? Anaxsa – put on your headphones. Lend me the danger lodged in your appliances.   Still warm, it hums
under your empty sky account   ripples it still sighs

LANDFALL

Time draws near. Notified in semaphore. The access approach, beware of
Too much. Backdoor ajar. By what authority does the sky address us thus?
What shape in this slot on a form for writing what? A portrait of waiting
back to back. The unproven conjecture of airports as doorways, regarding
herding capacity and habits.
Table manners.

Let down, let down the sky like mosquito netting

Under her dress is something
that matches the hotel decor
Mexican bordello style
its red
gathers and secures
all disclosure

It is red dictation
hand over mouth
the fullest speech blinded
speech   broad hand covers eyes
Sacrifice yet again, even do it to yourselves

from AERODROME ORION & Starry Messenger

Spin

in the flying city

firefly carrier

of pandemic

skirting the world as

the business of the day below the night withers the day

As the year continues   the daily life of incompletion

The dangerous life of

true north

and the eight directions of the compass

sighting surface wind without sensor

squall   funnel cloud

drifting blowing snow sand or dust

Heroic

Fog to the west

Severe turbulence and icing

thickening

beyond plot
Way beyond binoculars of plot

. . .

Hermes   Icarus   mid-air

freelance "spotters" for neighbourhood watch

watch smoke point
watch

Future infernos loom

Doubt born of the accretion of events
a silt

Cross talk   cross reference   cross continent   Rocking
horse entity casting aspersions   a slit

we must investigate the curse | cause
working something out in couplets

    quatrainally

diagonally ...   the form shall be in advance   an advance

   riveted

to closed circuit T.V.

/ < | \   _ _ - ~ ^^^^^^^^^ ` `

an eagle morphs into an advance concept vehicle
a swan into a child star
a daughter into a heap of land mines
Having misplaced the air
and at another time found it
having misrecognized the founding
as another kind of breathing

Dialing up the same cup

blood
  and blood line

Directions

mistaken for lighting at sunrise

shape's smoke appears

The poem is east

The poem is cast

drink Compliance

A 16th century speech is becoming on you

You wish

pilot deviations
runway incursions

a remunerating speech is required of you
ventriloquist for news anchors, stringers
tense lax harsh or leashed
falsetto colossal no matter
to the paver

The company hired a safety czar
The company hired an inspector general

who hushes the royal oracles

at adrenaline dawn

The company hired a weather clerk
The company hired a cloud catcher

The vertical state, a state, many a state
    remarking borders

Names in our nomenclature
for new species of exhaustion
Dear over-and-out do you speak Farsi at 3 a.m. our time

Flush of the wall under your sunrise
beneath our masked sleep
and the problem of distinguishing gas flares
from human settlements

The centipede aircraft carrier crawls brightly
over the 4 a.m. water

Prologue
[to be read in Aviation English]

A cadaver dog
and another dog

a talking corpse zipped up

for the duration in a
horsehair cocoon

and a baby just under
ripe   out with the wash

remarkable spectacles

1,   2   & 3

So many ways to
count the sky

Call to prayer

minaret terminal control

Elizabeth James & Frances Presley

from Neither the One
nor the Other

ups and ups
always the second syllable

bim-bo bim-bo bim-bo
and he said it's
sal-vo sal-vo sal-vo

applause & heavy rain save their appearances
I volley, though my nerve is broken –
there is no true spondee in English poetry

Pa   pa   pa   mime all plaudits
and reign savours volition
bite into the sprinkling of powder

a/men a/men a/men
underlined impatiently (he said)

(these are your words)

Ditch the index, ditch everything else and write something

a.m.

mirror and single
contact lens
tip o' my index
a reflex flinch
I put it in

mark lines
her eye eyes
poor authority
straight heir
clings to me

ma-
man
maudite

this is my ditch
the love is warty

mo
mor
morwyn
            (or

            if you prefer

            the breton morgan)

                sea
rising
                drift
ditch the index
love more than
                se
a monster

oh frances

morgan is my
mother

I do not   prefer

– scales aweigh!

it was those wide melodic leaps
she was scurrying rapidly
up and down the scales

eye-slash-lash scrape her swelled lid
nights after a taxing form filled dishabilly
            datasurge

ventures testing riotous finances
poetry day is worse than thought for the day

no upper body strength
no upper arm strength
no body-on-the-floor strength
no over-the-body strength
no under-the-body strength

she says that he says it's a dance about falling

really needing that time for herself but had to blame it on
no permit without kermit
and he says Yes but still my point
still   my   point

Ulli Freer was at VI
reading a sequence called dense
which includes the line

'there is no ego in collaboration'
it seemed egoistic to ask him about it

I also liked the line
'can't see the wood yet feel for the tree'
can't see the word
my elliptical Os
you have to see the word
        I mean the wood

and so we could –
fall for the trews
and creep to free

or prefer
singing together
of mount abora a a a

o labor –
it spurts, falutin
ab ovo
        a mon avis

We need to approach the pastoral with care and remember that it's not a convenient utpoa

                                        we need
                                  we need to approach
                              we need to approach the past
                          to approach the past we need we need
                                  to approach the pastoral
                          we need to approach the pastoral in a car
                              o approach the pastoral with care
                                  we read to poach the pastor
                                    to cart toward aporia
                          approach the waste and pare the weed to the core
                                    to catch a parsnip

                              and remember that it's not

and remember that it's not a convent
and remember that it's a con

ut poesia pastoralis

her oaks are tiny things in plastic tubes
like premature infants
sun catches their leaf shadow

the trees join heaven and earth
and the world below
on Blakean linear terms

I feel for their sinewed trunks
a muscular infold
cannot identify this tree

in the forms she remembers
from Nellie Nature

stock cubes / mach ants / chest hair

vend art / hew low / Lakes

fort sinus / Amis Larkin / tide history

for her : read-only : Neat-she

All the mythic versions of woman...
are consolatory nonsenses (Angela Carter: Sadeian Woman)

spiced parsnip   passive hole   lead detail
pound each   cut yew   broads
flat business   Hughes Morgan   post millennial
:   his entire (net) tribe of collectibles lodged here

(In terms of the travelogue, this is the (my) road to Norfolk.)

next morning I brought up the Sadeian Woman
and it quite put me off my sex

ni l'un ni l'autre   I do & I don't

his black weight on her calipered body
she said it was a girl's view but there must have been something
wrong in the phenomenon

The Sadeian Woman was Carter's vindication of the rights
she could have written a better book
given more time

   everything was showing
   as if showing was everything

   the chemise-en-scène
   her apparent
   parent
   rent

   a bone structure
   in repair

"original floor covering of tapestry embroidered by two of the
   princesses
4 ladies made a replica of it, which is identical but the colours are
   fresher of course
Osborne House, a real family home but some of the rooms were
   too opulent for my taste" (post card from my mother)

   everything was folded
   as if
   skirting the word in lime green
   her wainscot
   wave partition
   parted painted wagon

wains   coat

wains

       cot

Cottage my foot.

The palace to boot.

Queen Victoria had him brought to Osborne House, perhaps because filming would not be permitted at Balmoral.

I was sinking between Victoria's tyranny and Brown's paranoia. I had forgotten her reassuring banality.

Short breaks are available.

It's nice to have options at a bus stop.

A converted outbuilding the other side of the car port from the landlord's bungalow.

A controversial 135 feet high tent was raised over two acres of the town's holiday centre.

If the weather was bad I would read The Marginalization of Poetry.

When I had flu I read The Marginalization of Poetry.

'Mrs Brown' was taken by him to visit the poor in their own homes, laughing happily.

'Mrs Brown' was taken by him to her predictable, if politically sound, crockery.

Gratton Dale was full of bullfinches and goldfinches, and it had snowed on top of the mud.

We were somewhere on the Quantocks in the red river.

He also acted like an unpleasant bully.

She also acted like an unpleasant bully. Peel was forced to resign.

The females can be seen to have shorter sentences.

The male has a longer memory.

still the narrative unfolds one's sympathies shifting under his hairy
    blanket

*I couldn't help thinking that Cinderella was a touch more
traditional than Angela Carter's version.*

Hearing the bells at midnight we went to stand among the locals
outside the Duke of York.

Hearing bagpipes at midnight we joined the studio celebrities.

In exchange for Labour the cottar shall get access to the coterie.

It was not the widow's choice who she should remarry.

What might you have.

What might we have.

Finding it extremely hard to open up this poem again

Finding it extremely hard to open up

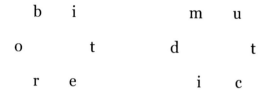

```
  b    i              m    u

o         t        d         t

  r    e              i    c
```

or bitten by blanket stitch
which is an orbiting style

running up against
all that joined up thinking
in the social exclusion unit

there is another clause
there is another cursive

*

tumulus umbrage dilates
cabled bearing borage

A little difference / making a great deal / different / interest rates /
fall by half / of one per cent / over / all over again

Can you credit / The Millennium / "our anniversary" / your
birthday, her / last ever PEP / We herd / Fortunes in floristry /
flow / owing

Seam non compliance will attract penalties
Food in your freezer
. Insure.

the word stress is less stable than you think
the women were all dressed in black tie
as Olive made a dash towards the subvocal
I like her line of suspension points
....

I struggle with my breath

Try the melismatic:

I str—u—u—u—u—gle

or ED:

I Struggle with my Breath

My mother could not catch her breath
I struggle to speak on their anniversary

dum dum dum dum b-dum dum dum dum

sing then, at
least sign

t tss   t tss   t tss   t tss

                             listen
oh mother we love you ~~get up~~

Lisa Jarnot

from Some other kind of mission

Part One

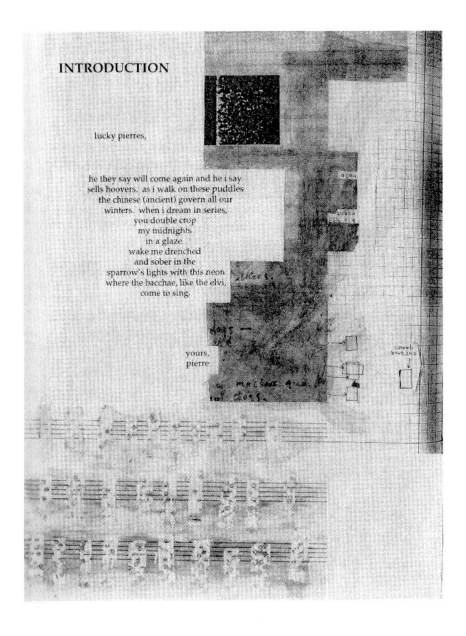

INTRODUCTION

lucky pierres,

he they say will come again and he i say
sells hoovers. as i walk on these puddles
the chinese (ancient) govern all our
winters. when i dream in series,
you double crop
my midnights
in a glaze.
wake me drenched
and sober in the
sparrow's lights with this neon
where the bacchae, like the elvi,
come to sing.

yours,
pierre

Part Four

Because we first met under false pretenses it is
no longer clear to me that you and i are now working
in a supermarket or that i formerly worked in a super-
market which included a dream about a thunderstorm.
Because i was so drunk this morning and tomorrow,
forgive me please. Because of nothing, one year and
a half ago i know that people have named some pieces
of the body and a lot more. Because I don't know your
phone number this letter has a lot of mistakes and i was
not able to buy even chicken in a supermarket. Because
i meet you or you meet me in traditional uniforms where
i enjoy my time and your best friend Paul, like syrup,
never again. Because i hope so you know that the spring
is coming, and the ocean, so what?

Part Four

Against the sun. a dream of source against the sun. willed against untitled. it is only a dream of the lawn. blowing against the source of the sun. due east. a dream against the source of the sun in the dream due east. count meticules. find. find visible. find dream of the sun it is only. in going to the median. meridian source the sun goes means. meridian dreams of means. find. find visible. find means. find dream due east. find means of. if. in find the means go east the median source of dream support in east due means supports the sun in find in visible in in click. in dreams of. it is only. going. in the. in find. after. of. is. only. going. in the. due east. of of of.

Part Nine

And then we accidentally blew up a gas station in virginia. miles of strips of pig. my love speaks like the chickens in the blue light by the cape. my love speaks like the jets of grain. my love speaks like the ivy in the hence field. then we filled the salad bar unlike the sails of boating in the struct. siege perilous. there was an earl hight grip. there was an early grip of seized and hurled the grip. last night i dreamt. and in his collar by the bridge. of habits in the meantime.

Part Six

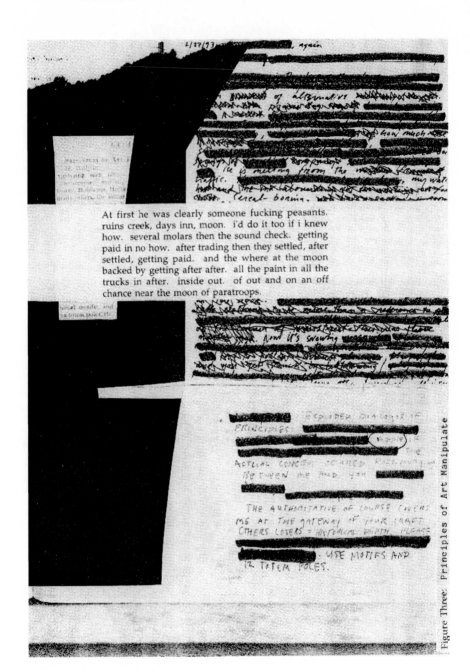

At first he was clearly someone fucking peasants.
ruins creek, days inn, moon. i'd do it too if i knew
how. several molars then the sound check. getting
paid in no how. after trading then they settled, after
settled, getting paid. and the where at the moon
backed by getting after after. all the paint in all the
trucks in after. inside out. of out and on an off
chance near the moon of paratroops.

Figure Three: Principles of Art Manipulate

from Ring of Fire

Poem Beginning with a Line by Frank Lima

And how terrific it is to write a radio poem
and how terrific it is to stand on the roof and
watch the stars go by and how terrific it is to be
misled inside a hallway, and how terrific it is
to be the hallway as it stands inside the house,
and how terrific it is, shaped like a telephone,
to be filled with scotch and stand out on the street,
and how terrific it is to see the stars inside the radios
and cows, and how terrific the cows are, crossing
at night, in their unjaundiced way and moving
through the moonlight, and how terrific the night is,
purveyor of the bells and distant planets, and how
terrific it is to write this poem as I sleep, to sleep
in distant planets in my mind and cross at night the
cows in hallways riding stars to radios at night, and
how terrific night you are, across the bridges, into
tunnels, into bars, and how terrific it is that you are
this too, the fields of planetary pull, terrific, living
on the Hudson, inside the months of spring, an
underwater crossing for the cows in dreams, terrific,
like the radios, the songs, the poem and the stars.

Brooklyn Anchorage

and at noon I will fall in love
and nothing will have meaning
except for the brownness of
the sky, and tradition, and water
and in the water off the railway
in New Haven all the lights
go on across the sun, and for
millennia those who kiss fall into
hospitals, riding trains, wearing
black shoes, pursued by those
they love, the Chinese in the armies
with the shiny sound of Johnny Cash,
and in my plan to be myself
I became someone else with
soft lips and a secret life,
and I left, from an airport,
in tradition of the water
on the plains, until the train
started moving and yesterday
it seemed true that suddenly
inside of the newspaper
there was a powerline and
my heart stopped, and everything
leaned down from the sky to kill me
and now the cattails sing.

from Black Dog Songs

On the Sublime

They loved these things. Giraffe,
they loved giraffe. They loved the
concept of the tapir. They loved
him, wholly unnamed. They loved
competence and they loved the
dark metallic stapler. They loved
to trace the trajectory of the
armadillo. They loved to speak of
plankton. They also loved the fog.

On the Lemur

That they loved to go on unmistaken, that they loved
to not to be gratuitous or cry, that they loved the
fortitude of yaks, that suddenly they loved the whiskey
and the sunlight and the key, that they loved the corn
cow and the cow corn that it ate, that they loved the cat
food as it rolled across the floor, that they liked and
loved the coffee that was warm inside the day, that
they loved the sound of hail and what it broke, that
they knew they loved the river that was made where
people dream, that they loved the loins of lions and of
lambs, that they loved confusion and the tools,
that they loved the whistle of the evening train, that they
loved the drugs they dreamt they loved and took inside
the dreams, that they loved their pictures taken and the
sides of barns, that they loved all outer space.

from Night Scenes

Man's Fortunate Feast
For Mendy

The fatigue of feast,
the umbrellas and the
suits and ties, the
thunder of it,
floating into panther
fatness full
the checkmarks
that accompany the page
the gluttony of flower prints,
the tight skin of the sterile pear
gone spawned, consumed,
in leaf

no more lamb chops for you,
no more scrambled eggs and greens,
no more aardvark statues,
no more American flags,
no more caterpillars to
torch out of the trees,
cut wood, dead wood,
white pine branches,
drooping cypri,
dog asleep under the brush
also gone,
sun gone in the gray
swimming hole a stage prop,
water from the creek
feeding agile garlic greens in May

whose wallet, whose welfare,
whose heart, whose feathers,
whose darkness is the
darkness of a missing bird,
a tunnel of mind, an income of
herbaceous bruise, who is
and who is not, voracious
braeken gone.

Christine Kennedy

from Hobby Horse:
A Puppet Play for Cabaret Voltaire

ACT 3
A Puppet Extravaganza

Meine Damen und Herren, Ladies and Gentlemen, Mesdames et Messieurs
The company of puppets is assembled for tonight's show.

A Field Ballet for Armed Personnel
The characters in order of appearance are as follows:

>   The Wound Puppets
>   The Wound Puppets are a troupe sculpted from anti-matter
>   Their limbs are the cone and cylinder negative spaces of bullet paths
>
>   The Field Doctor
>   The Field Doctor is made of hollowed out gutter splints and valves
>
>   The Calf and the Sheep
>   These are made of leather and wool and have silk leads

Dance 1, for the Wound Puppets, entitled
"The Bullet Entry"

[There is a clear aperture of entry]

The company divides on the stage
fragments without splintering

Movements are more sedentary than propelled
kept together by the articular surface

Long fissures in the articulation do not radiate

There is a narrowness of the capsular

The solos are slight traumatisms of the bullets still present

The dance concludes with a favourable evolution of wounds

Dance 2, for the Wound Puppets and the Field Doctor, entitled "The Diagnosis"

The wound puppets take up
the position the wounded man occupies
at the moment of traumatisation

There are changes of shape in the limbs

There is abnormal mobility

Wounded men still manage to move the joints

Immobilisation must be carried out

They must abstain from any exploration

For each articulation
the fissures take the directions forced on them

Dance 3, for the Wound Puppets and the Field Doctor, entitled "The Treatment"

Continual *pas de deux* of Field Doctor with each Wound Puppet

Immobilisation of limbs during treatment
leaving articulation free

There is incision and
a burrowing of the pus

The articulation should be washed out

There is the application of dressings

Passive movements begin early

The Wound Puppets moved earliest move the most
those moved later lose power

Dance 4, for the Wound Puppets, the Field Doctor, the Calf and the Sheep, entitled "Wounds of the Nerves"

Tenacious, intermittent or continuous
spasm and contraction
awakened by the slightest contact
and more so in a fear of contact

Sensori-motor disturbances
interrupted, forced back

The Calf and Sheep enter

The Field Doctor ties them to the Wound Puppets by leads of silk threads

They all dance together while leading the animals from the stage

[Aperture of exit]

from Twelve Entries from The Encyclopaedia of Natural Sexual Relations

green leaves with gold veins.
are also
ANO – Everg
in sprin
sand.
summer
tam 60
perature
A, re
another sp
ANO
Evergre
gardens
house.
A.g
laurel-li
flowers.
ANT
Ear.-
sunny
Useful
Plant au
division
A.di
A.d.
I in.
ANT
MILE-
Borders
suitable
mon Ch
Tea. T
when in
Propa
seed so
A. bi
mer; I-
A. no
White,
A. tinctoria - yellow, August; 2ft.

VOLUME 1
The spore pustules of chrysanthemum rust
gardens grown, but mostly for their
green leaves with gold veins. There
where the Borders seed in old soils
springs a perfectly
Evergre
A.di
A, re
A. bi
A, di
ANO A.no
he corms

suitable White flowers are also Borders
Plant au table for mon Ch laurel-li

no vision in gardens
but in division

soil White flowers there
or Plant seed in green veins
perfectly old

grown, but mostly for their ornamental

There A.Lilliago - White, July-August;
June –
ly-za),
perfectly
ed 5 in.
ndy soil,
he corms
old soils
embles a
cies most
thoxan -
- Hardy
table for
ng. Pro-
where the
vision in
is - cus),
used for
Seed can
n; but in
a south
uring the
r-ium),
s suitable
spring in
phagnum
rt of the
- August
- March,
brids are

dissolved in water at the rate of	the affected trees should be sprayed	
1lb. to		:
the s		w
etc., ar	**VOLUME 6**	s
Poisonin	*115. Raspberry beetle grub*	;
of no us	When are proprietary	
tissues	Poisons dissolved in us?	i-
juices or		is
therefor	When curled i	e
directly	is almost u	's
is nicot	of no us	is
1½ oz.		x,
it is ex		e.
may be	There may be the sex hour	-
chips, 1	the spray print of water	e
of wate		r
half the	There the sex	er
hour, th	is water	is
in fresh		
Mix the	apply this wash directly	e
to 10 ga		r
wash is	be concentrate	h
spray pr	to affected waters	g
get a fir		e.
curled i	be mixed in half	t
almost u	the spray of any hour	a
as requir		e
When		t
are prese	The Mix of fresh juices of tissues	g-
of lead		r-
of the	half the wash is of lead	n
in any o	trees of fine curled lead	i-
of the di	dissolved in us	le
be mixed		y
concentra		g
There		-
proprietary pesticides on the	portant to apply it as a very fine	

The Fruit Group of the R.H.S is flourishing, and membership is open
to any Fell   ons,
and althou   ere
seems no r
 Model f   the
spring of n   on;
there are   and
Kew Gard   our
public par   **VOLUME 8**   bles
for the sch   *111. Brown rot on plum*
 ADVICE   cultural ADVICE through fruit
have fruit   and
gardeners   plant these apple trees   stic
of through   to Demonstrate cultural Models   lly,
Horticultu   ty's
cultural   orti-
Demonstra   gardeners depart to dig ice and plant   ice.
provided   they remember spring provided other help   ally
promised.   e is
although   ion,
                      rules for fruit promised Law
                        our tree promised these

                   If Fruit Fell there may open
                        other flourishing

                       transplant any ally
 Tenants   plant other rules
plant fruit   they
with the u   help
Law, and   -at-
remember   t be
rules; in p   egal
the depart   and
satisfactor   ore
than to   ent
litigate.
  If I plant apple and other tree fruits may I dig these up and transplant them,

med with "carpet
beddin
thickly
patter
works
to fill a
amoun
to mai
severe
style 1
counte
apart
public
large p
dens, b
except
quite a
howeve
well b
the s
garden
79),
often
unlove
of bits
  The
tional s
plot g
lent re
forma
hered t
plest so
a bird-
on a s
surrou

VOLUME 10
Scale on camellia leaf
The plot
so thickly formational with unlove

In a public garden
of severe style

strips maidens
soils bedding
fills the well

be a broad
quite apart
and bordered by counter works

bordered by narrow strips of soil   or broad and short, or square. In

Myung Mi Kim

from Commons

Exordium

In what way names were applied to things. Filtration. Not every word that has been applied, still exists. Through proliferation and differentiation. Airborn. Here, this speck and this speck you missed.

Numbers in cell division. Spheres of debt. The paradigm's stitchery of unrelated points. What escapes like so much cotton batting. The building, rather, in flames. Does flight happen in an order.

Dates to impugn and divulge. The laws were written on twelve tablets of bronze which were fastened to the rostra. Trembling hold. Manner of variation and shift. Vacillation hung by tactile and auditory cues.

Those which are of foreign origin. Those which are of forgotten sources. Place and body. Time and action. The snow falls. A falling snow. A fallen snow. A red balloon and a blackwinged bird at semblance of crossing in a pittance of sky.

Chroniclers enter texts and trade. Was to children dying before their mothers. Accounts and recounting. A nation's defense. Names of things made by human hands. Making famine where abundance lies.

Mapping needles. Minerals and gems. Furs and lumber. Alterations through the loss or transposition of even a single syllable. The next day is astronomical distance and a gnarled hand pulling up wild onion.

Lamenta

229

The transition from the stability and absoluteness of the world's contents to their dissolution into motions and relations.

P: Of what use are the senses to us – tell me that

E: To indicate, to make known, to testify in part

Burning eye seen

Of that

One eye seen

bo-bo-bo   k-k-k

Jack-in-the-pulpit   petaling

To a body of infinite size there can be ascribed neither center nor boundary

say . siphon

Sign scarcity, the greeting – *have you eaten today?*

Signal of peonies   singing given to bullfrogs

Give ear to the quarrels of the marketplace

When the wheel (A) was turned, the gate (B) was raised, thus allowing
water to flow from (C) to (D), giving clearance for the ship to pass beneath

lever   .   girt

Host and parasite

Implicated armed band

Where would one live

A custom of wrapping the head in willow branches

311

Hours whose length varied with seasons

Hours held by mechanical clock

An abstract metric to gauge daily time

Compendium to dispersals of currency

Farm and factory, bank and municipality

travel   .   athwart

what would identify the speakers of the idiom

312

Woodness and continual waking

Raging stretching and casting

Now chanting now weeping

The medicine is that the head be shaved, washed in lukewarm vinegar

The forehead anointed with the juice of lettuce or of poppy

If the woodness lasts three days without sleep, there is no hope of recovery

"war-torn"

"turbulent homeland"

All that we see could also be otherwise

All that we can describe could also be otherwise

The thing seen is the thing seen together with the whole space

318

Their [brilliance and their dependence]

Flowers [gladiolas, zinnia, delphinium]

Offset the houses

What the bluejay exacts [upside down]
[inside] the half-broken sunflower, pecking

Scrip – a small purse carried by a pilgrim, shepherd, or beggar

One among fled many
                    felt

Any different tissue constitutes a heterology

White light after breath (circling the mouth)//

The baby asleep in the house
And two figures down by the barn

It burns. Membrane.

Further carbonization of matter

bellrag   ㅈ
bellslip   ─
                     jw

322

Terms stringent for lack of food

Root insect berry pass a mud inscription

Place where

Weeks of slaughter and remonstrance

Fed the children and animals first

Without interruption the entry log of days

Snow may be falling

405

Little flower,

What day is it

The light stops at glum

O'clock and f

A rain saturated tree trunk becomes a feeling

The city of one's birth and the people inside it

415

War is there and travel

The same is my sister, brothers, and mother

The father is thrush, white at birth and at dusk

Father is burying ground cool to the touch

This is some color but what color is it

"left their homes after two solid days of attacks"

"they had stayed to take care of their cow"

"the extreme cold froze medicine"

"religion and capitalism intersect in the muddy village twenty miles north of"

426

jiph-jiph-jiph

Swallow Swallow Bird

This is the gullet

Helmets make cooking pots

Tin cans make roofs

[sparrow, crow]

Not much left
Not much left

502

To bring to a close

What is to do
What is to happen

Frances Kruk

from Down you go, or, Négation de bruit

I

Swarms!
we will bang
into the sun Blinded

thirsty,
howling

III

Subterranean gallery & the fist
against deaf walls

glittering, the mine shaft
dumb, the hands

IV

Bound underground on Hooks
you put the holes in
the dream Head,
drill geometry,

six claw solitaire forever

V

I was or am
in the chasm
refracted though the dream had shut.

crkl hard. mauve.
In the passage, Tiny dogs on ice all round Tiny, Tiny
dogs

& howls

VII

The most Pathetic poem is small people on fire

VIII

How stupid it is to wait.

Machines & truth shall be crushed by water
or something surging Nervous walls
with their cheap metal flickers

my Machine. your flicker.

IX

Again the fake garden, motionless plastic curves.
This time we are Great in our Smart
Bomb Time Machine device.

We come to fuck the mutants
We go to mutant them
I am with the mutant
firing limbs

X

Back in the mines
the dwarves, the presences

Spinning silent

Your mouth doesn't
move but there is no word

XI

There's a boat & it has dead noise
& there, in sand you hear dead
noise, revolt noise.
Negation of noise
unheard

XII

Mouths bitter in sand.

I ordered a hurricane & I am still
on this island I am still
on this island

XIII

The waiting area bleached
the pitiless colour of provisional crimes.

then waves of brutal as Cochlea
at high pressure Crush, listen:

Radio, when it's not human

XIV

White water white light
Storm on the inner island

– but I'm

XV

The final duct & its shards of condensation
ringing Metal My chest
judder I
want the aerofoils for this last

wait, Exile! I have no
eyes, I feel no
wind

XVI

All round that glittering penalty
a Gel of True holds the wettest
crkl

if there are wires they must be
stilled they must be Stripped
their pulse plastinate

XVII

That passage moving open –

we inserted a history & now it won't stop

XVIII

Ends will not leave alone & so Heads are taken
put in water
floods water sense water talks water
When I Name It

XX

the orchids are fake, stupid fake island & the forest
the forest mythic behind orchids
it has no songs. like Minerals at Night
there is no depth

Francesca Lisette

from
sub-rosa, or, The Book of Metaphysics

Part 1: In Thrall

THE MOON'S MOVE

March indescribable devolving into a factotum, a.
A private museum. Strangled cords melt the
precise flesh of friends/ pop-eye filth
gathering in a steam world, hub of
purpling ticks. You knock me sideways
crescent across the table not speaking to
disturbs the present's slow curl of disease.

Wipe back foot after coming
home lazy, in defeat
where do the skies fit
under all this we into & rubber.

Last time I lay down it was to lie next to you.
Dubbed whyte feminism punk road movie
shut out a calling card who soaps tarot speech
anatomy bundle, she says, but famish or pick
at a waiting clit.

FED ON SCARLET HIPS

My lover's thoughts are not
                    of me at all.
                              – John Wieners

Decorticated, time is deliquescent
echolocation.

Eternity sprung back ineluctably thru
my lover's lips

Hush
& stagger   across
  softly spoken ways.

Time-stuck
  fool's paradise
sings in the fabric of
your skin

Borne, a studded
bird-mass is loaded w/
fortune primaries,
fruit of a thousand
sorrows.

My heart is a clip
for speaking with.

LANGUAGE LANGUAGE LANGUAGE LANGIUGE LANGAUGE

Embryo spoiled
in a dark bleat of snow.
What lives in a wrinkled
condom
  Mine.

WINE & ROSES

The fast losses of an hour. Your blue disturbia in the sunshine
& amitriptyline coating sags, mixing the green and the brown.
Detach speaking cord and wrap around dogs
who are not us,
leafed and debarred. Costco Amy
weeps. What is to weep. Is to Ophelia'z
drownin dress blooms. Discordance
can make you happy, can make a joke
of death. Living thinks you. The trying-
to is actually beautiful.

*

Weakness a problem for art. During fashion
artifice is set afloat on a membrane of safety
for locks' quavers. Indiscernible trouble
around the lower mandibular gums. The recesses

get caught in a tongue. One is hardly at a
pertinence to explain
gestures under office. Is a flesh a loot
undived.

*

Quarrel me hearts to set aflame in evening's
slow glare or a ribcage yanks off an ear
& is a child again, luring out frolics
for shame. Love is not a breathing thing
Smirched with sighs, until it walks out
alone. The house I lived with turns
to a clatter of nature sounds neither
done or retrieved.
Ague mental.

*

Vulnerability is specificity, or anything
plays into the question of trust
remaindered in darkness, where sickling
angels capsize & spread. Eleven eleven
: lust in foreground enmity is barrier
broke, disconnect sugaring leaves in layers.
Promise me, sailor? – that only reality strips
bare feet with hot tarmac and shit under
my fingernails, from loving you
keep only what I can't touch
winter's ecstasy behind.

THE WOMEN

After Anna Mendelssohn

the women. move in terse quatrains
  arms relinquishing logic, dairy talk oval
splintered the impossible frames writ as hooks
  for gendered language is outside the matrix platform
post – : viability as an unquestioned subject, the politics
of yr performance consist of a picked chicken bone exiting
your mouth. morse code swells the stitches in lines
  pimps are short on counterfactual

anyway, do not deny
  you woke up with a cigarette in your mouth when you
shifted/ pray to satire spit doesn't come clean, the holes
are not vanishing points, drunk emissary pretties milk
of the system but eyes are lucid: heart-felt-shouting
what do to that
it is not simple, stapled human participle in half-time
                                        energy flow

TUSK-RIDDEN

sometimes always. the virgin is

step out w/ panels stretched wingform

corrective vision untrammelled
burden stringing intransigent global cosmetic
standard, yet gospel skeleton is restive in the wind.
formless *reductio*: opacity blurred for
tonic privacy
& breathe again, waxy carrier entrusts
a pagan restorative birth ritual
discloses not emphatic fish anomie of
gentle lung; scissoring its own pain,
plural windows replicating the retreated stars.
not wholly this.
a spot holds
co-existing plates to account, shyness
fault shared. occasionally
it flickers into my consciousness that it is
 one of 7 billion, not folding its
 insignificance into a hurtless line
(the line is clear) rather gutted into maintenance,
non-insistent cupole for cascading sentience
 is a spark, despite
interrupted will surfeiting each
midnight's dance
 a final day. hands shiver in time to situated prisons
 & disorder returns over the silent and black trees.

Part 2: Becoming

I.

Writing. Out of the birth inamorata that shelters me.
I: cleansed. I communicate from parallel data density
socket. Eye: alright. Eye definitive K-Mart complex.
I here, touched, where technology is abandoned. I,
falling aboard. Eye rope in the primacy of winter
daylight. Numb wash of keen swallows pound the face.
I : citric water. I : dissolved into acid counts. Unhook
the temerity of walking as matched shore to shore.
Your belly goes against me like a bruise, or garbage
sack spilling. Repeat: dispenser. Repeat: the sexual
gap of your mouth (a dark rose) – love/bloody spittle/vomit.
We constitute ourselves as liquid rubber running through
the town's tar pits. Isolated: lassitude. Hairy numbers
come crawling out with the populace's skulls between
their teeth. River: rivulet. Scarlet flesh of a shell notated
& hollowed by grim virgin birth itemised 1st para. Not the
hole I dwell in: love–blood–vomit. Prise open the can
with a gear shift & swap genitalia albeit monkey surprise
glove excitement. The story's O couldn't rid me of
glossolalia no matter how hard they tried. I sang on,
vowels cresting a unintelligible glass. Cracked laminate:
the Duchy. Failed omniscience hunts to gloss panda, we.
Once were. Animals hindered by subject lines &
multiple proclivities. Every time I try to be funny
or clever my body screams so I have to stop. I have
to sacrifice my need for love or the abuse known as
interpretive approval. The body beautiful, the sunk
navigator tuned to inner anchor. Now then the body
flames it shrieks it hovers it blasts it's been plundered
by years, animations, shit, flows. Unhindered by
sustenance, attacked for entertainment, & now
surfaces in the grass before a waiting smile.

[DISTANCING, objects]

...the sky unrelenting at an impasse.
The sun moved inside of her & died.
It seemed every object was a vehicle
for great tempests of rhetoric & sound.
Every second dug into her.
Plates of skin unfolded.
Faces dissolved in rage colour.
Dim clutchings at semantics would scatter.
A knife expanded with a flick of tongue.
Heart's-ease unceasing.
The gap in the muscles goes, 'POP'.
Sipping the ocean's bowl complicates each manoeuvre.
I feel sure the syntax is rusting out of use.
Minutes of recalibration wink anonymous tower essences.
Time is over a barrel.
The fish inside appear silent, but are shouting
To fortify their solitude with war.
A motivator drawing its finger across the lens.
How do you know where the sky starts.
Perhaps it is touching your skin.

III.
I pierced a whale-song with our living, manufactured
in the sobriety of Discontent. Candied language
brewing in stuck tics – nose the tide you take me for.
Disembodied disembarked. The wind waves a little
dive over the cut finger, convenient Neanderthal
flesh gets gulped by the dream of the living.
As though poetry is where it's really "at".
Lilac scales drip out of the dreaming mouth: fish
oracle. Window daughter divines an exclamation mark
out of NO PRISON out of unclaimed time. And the

solarised cup smashes on the tinder of our wanting
unknown & precise & beautiful though we keep
it to ourselves, like we hardly reveal to each other
the frill of our cunts. Pale plastic saints of blind
asking. How do oranges levitate on water. A room
is a planet a heart is a dildo an alabaster is a torn
strip running. Endless whys make up our childhood
& we've forgotten the answers. Sun nudges his
vertebrae into a flower rodded with pink inferno
smear. Elastic breathes a taut sigh, as we do.
We = forced to sup a brawl lament. We =
stacked on knowledge gaping. The index turns
& whirs: ah energetic starting again with each
morning ah self-index recovering from a blunt
line. Creep across the earth in full bliss-ignorance,
too starved to fake it. I am only ever the blue throttle
                    when she comes through me
              shinning my guts like so many solar panels
Flash of silver Eyes & hard engagement she rinses all
intensity with her own pearl blankness, engorged
with flowers & riding over the dashed day with hooks
for frowns with sallow weeds for trophies with poverty
for aces with battered words for armour, she is bound
to charge across each of our faces at the battle-lines,
unrecognized in flame

Sophie Mayer

from Her Various Scalpels

No Such Thing

"Les travellings sont affaires de morale."
                                        Jean-Luc Godard, 1960

Filmgrimage

> [Earliest use in English, 1205. From Old Fr. *Pelegrin*. From Latin
> *peregrinum*, one who comes from foreign parts. *Per* (through) +
> *ager* (fields, lands). Wanderer, religious traveler, colonist, falcon]

wander through the [visual] field
travel with film in mind

Montréal

Pèlerinage. Film is a foreign land we come through.
A foreign land where we come to.

We confuse the places we dreamed with the places we walk.
They lie over one another, a slender archaeology.

If I stand on the right corner and look, I will step in through
the lens of the camera.
                                        Aperture.
Yes. An opening. Opening something in me.
                                        Open. But empty.
The film? It's all around us.
                                        The place. The church. Like a tomb.
So much to see...
                        Nothing. At the tomb of the film the body was gone.

Glasgow

The city / screen takes on
a double meaning:

Entrance.
Refuse.

The screen a
window barred.

There is no outside
Only frames within frames.

Paris

You write to me from the end of cinema. I see it: the leader
winding through the projector, clicking like a stone against
pavement. Love is a film that takes hold of the city: the screen
will tear. Can you see the space that will show? Such questions,
like kisses, leave me breathless.

Iceland

It is so cold that speech is impossible. The landscape breathes
words of ice and fire. With picks and maps, we go
looking. See signs. *Here Be Monsters*. Geysirs. Glaciers. Volcanoes.

Rainbows. Cinema speaks in signs: each can be mined
for meaning. The landscape is impossible. With fire and ice,
it writes and erases the story. Here be angles, edges, frames.

Teeth chattering, we approach. See films
in the Northern Lights. Myth, riddle, rune. Score
images on bone. Mouth strange songs sung to drums.

Let them escape on our breath when we wake.

Two Scenarios for Short Films

Je Suis Ici

Intro: driving through vineyards. Music: Edith Piaf. Jaunty.
Where are we? *Ici*. Here. At last. After
here in my phrase book: hot. House.
                              Then hungry.

1. A mountain village.
I am learning the words of things: *montagne,*
magasin. Fermé . Still a shop when it's closed?
The street is empty with. *Pierres. Chiens. Soleil.*
Comprenez-vous français? I wish I knew the French
                              for swallow.

2. A market.
Marché. Also, *marcher*: to walk. *Ça marche bien.*
It goes well. I walk. My stride rhythmic:
Bien. Rien. Can you eat a smell? A taste?
                              A place?

3. A pristine untouched salad.
Plat: a plate or meal. But more.
Art, the placement *comme ça*. Angles. Muscles. Flesh.
Fresh. Untouched. If I eat, will this be *ici*
                              forever?

4. Van Gogh Café, Arles.
Days proceed by frames: windows (car, hotel, café).
By guidebook, painting, memory, viewfinder, postcard.
Frame. *Fermé*. Everything here seen a million times.
                              Take it.

5. Looking through cards with a pot of salt to hand.
Sel. Once currency. Pot of gold to stop
meat from turning. Like love: keeps things fresh,
red and present. Fire. Running through me –
freshwater worth its salt. A day's grain (or
grace). Its taste. The touch of it to
                     my tongue.

6. Salt mountains seen from a fortress whose shadow on ramparts looks like teeth.
Bite into blue. Make dents. Impossible. Untouchable.
All I have wanted: sky, sun. To see
the frame. And beyond it. To open
the eyes of my brightest wings and turn
                     my face

7. She licks the stamp and places it on the blank card before posting.
                     (in)to the sun.

from (O)

All about Suffrage was Taught under Mrs. Catt's Direction

Or, Djuna Barnes reports from the trial of Pussy Riot.

I've come from the side of the world. I've been on the underside of the watch.
I've been breast-to-breast with the ticks.

> Even the air in Russia causes pain to us!
> This is what happens when you touch an abscess ready to burst!
> You struck against the very snakes' nest which has now attacked you!

Glimpses in the Condensed Course of Two Weeks, where all about suffrage was
taught under Mrs. Catt's direction.

> When I am powerless, I am strong.
> We are against Putin's chaos.
> Orthodox culture might also be on the side of civil revolt.

Girls who grew old in a year.

> Only when they weighed up the political and symbolic damage that we
> had inflicted with our art did they decide to protect society against us
> and our conviction.
> Prison is Russia in miniature.
> We are freer than all those who sit opposite us on the side of the
> prosecutor, because we can say what we please, and we do.

The stage was a thing of the future, and future possibilities at work on it: a vivid
gehenna!

> That is how this complicated punk adventure ended.
> Where should the blame lie for the performance in the Christ the
> Saviour Cathedral and the subsequent trial? It lies with the
> authoritative nature of the political system.
> I am extremely angered by the phrase 'so-called' which the State
> Prosecutor uses to refer to contemporary art. This trial is just a so-
> called trial!

They were not naughty songs, mademoiselle; they were life –
They were the little pen knife blade with which one cuts the wrist of malice and
deceit.

> Religion was in opposition then.
> They spat on our outstretched hand – They shouldn't have.
> I am not afraid of you.

Oh, dear Lord, what have we done to receive so much beauty per flash!

Note: All offset quotations are from the trial statements made by Maria Alyokhina,
Yekaterina Samutsevich, and Nadezhda Tolokonnikova during their trial, as translated
by Sasha Dugdale. All other material is quoted from Djuna Barnes' journalism, as
collected in ed. Douglas Messerli, *Poe's Mother*.

from TV GIRLS

what is (this) birth
    but a state
        of emergency

state: of
    as colonial imposition
    for the record
    in writing
    your name
    I'm in

loving this?

NO
    //
        kneel

as knuckles are bones, kneel

*

all you need is a girl & a gun
all you need is a girl & a guitar
all you need is a white horse at dusk with panic in its teeth
all you need is that dirt in your mouth
all you need is
precipitation // the precipitating
incident :: drop
        droplet
        dropped
        dropping

  & sudden ::
        cascade   (of)
all you need // it sings   in distortion
            in   slow motion
      in   m   ineral t   i   m   e

INTERIOR. NIGHT.

SHE raises her weapon
                    voice

*

fall
        kneel
fall
        funereal
fall
        tenebral
fall
        tenacity
fall
        water
fall
        open
foll
        ow
full
        of
all

Carol Mirakove

from Occupied

i'm not human.

+

parting from the underlake & a little weak

beaten moon, vernacular wrappings –
hands up, & exit
slowly.
addict sounds the door in love.
how many poems called dreams?
the long walk,
the waking life.

spirit of the night light hangs
another step.

+

why not aim
what is life:
in this world
if not you

+

proof

there is no

fundamental difference:

everybody looks the same

in here these bloody clothes

from Mediated

you a walking forest   me with city smoke

it makes little sense to not be complex, muting in an ear leaves
chained an archived document to
affront
shellac   she is susceptible to faith.

what you are – found – collective
in discovery
from chaos
          factories?   labor doesn't live here anymore
                    float
                    problem   the eliminal   human

                                        Cassandra the future
                                        she'd wake up
                                        a core dump
                                        departure does this work?

                                        for you?

                                        you must choose?

                                        sides? apparently you break

                                                          Where is
                                                    the remote?

                                                          control?

[stick figure with gun]

      neither done nor gone I can feel   (the sun)
like I'm speaking white subtitles
on a bleached-out film
       strip "plastic poetry"
they sing
"que sera, sera"
& in a store
front they
paint "© yourself"
an icon in the laminate
suicide
      to feign
      in balance warped
      & feel like
         a liar put
      a place
      in place

a synapse
      extinguished & cheered
         a santé
./smack.sh
a face she
      comes at a
         cost & they are coming :
            disembodied in parades
      were to perish
in and in
         an underestimation
         of what I might love

      "we are the cause of hunger"

your mouth is right & pins
down my uncertainty

for pain in the world
for joy in the world
for currents we channel

anguish
desires
a causal body

with one hand on your back
and another in a tunnel

passing through invoked
caverns & conscious
                faults
        inadequately humbled
        taken
        to freefall
                & firmly
        abandon
in the forcefully captured
present, precisely
        to view | history
                        the bondage of karma
                        the dripping
branches
breaking
        out of the carriage &
                        looking
                                up
        tensegrity
                tangled we might be
sin:
we live without.
shooting
in a bigbad
babybird
sky

IT HAS GOTTEN HARD

to say   [DYNAMITE]   anything
we eat too fast for arguments, geometry
evidence (equals) brute force cropped
images amplified I agree & medicated
would you like some spinach with your
chemicals counterpoint to human interest
content beyond the strip-mall :: t   a   b   o   o
the ELF on SUVs rapt bandana deed
extreme

quite a conundrum   in which

I can neither [slit] throats nor slip in vague
submissions   [*I'm   OK   You're   OK*]
WHO   IS   G   O   O   D
or what limp truce
                              remaindered?
exasperated of the cross-hair rocker love evangeline
two wrongs don't make a right it takes a multitude
regurgitating litigiousness has Kevin Bales
repeatedly booked forced to fear libel, numbered
    world arrests / a lattice in common
                f o o d   a n d   d e c e n c y

gypsy in us seen this subtle light can tent bang bang

WE NEED TO TALK

do normative ethics make sense to you?
I'm coming down on the side
of description. how is your money factors into morals
'meta-' seems so FDR-era & so, so we meet again – in
moral indignation, baby needs new shoes, mountain
needs a pipelay, bully needs an ego –   w e l l
we move on
phoenix, similar to earth / streets repent we plant esteem
& lay claims like farmers we revere I till

a plaster ~~chain store~~. analog illiteracy
my daily happenstance removed with good intentions.
who doesn't spin in synaesthesia?

justified?   sufficient?

I try conscientiousness & dusted
hands that I have learned to use type dam
                                divisions
                    staking claim & stroking calm & in this
state
                    your ardent mandates, e.g.,

                    vote FOR WHAT or die? for what?

          consensus   what I mean.

love kills hate

I can make myself older
       drug-ready   star coupon
    beauty map when words
            come before energy
I round my whole
            mouth & take
      the nearest train

      without faces   we   we can have faces
      without names we   we can have names

fable the red
    flag & elsewhere Vieques
              forgetting there's a fire
          escape   pollution
                     as progress
                 busted like pictures

      in Bolivia they said   plant rice
      is high-fructose corn syrup
      not more offensive
      than the coca leaf?
            "I don't need a bag"

sat   as was expected
of a dog   begged
as was expected   of a dog
ate scraps   pooped
        & slept

            a face shield
            a shell game
            a hole is a tunnel

     happy in our habits every
           body   costume   drop

reconciling Nietzsche's line,

"if you stare into the abyss,
it stares back at you"
                    sprouting   it is prudent
                          to have faith

                          from every integer,
                          insect, indigene, import
                          from every inter-
                          dependent a people

on our streets that
might our bodies
move

                forget what bores you

                          in this ring
                          burn bright not out

                this bridge
                is us
                this love
                kills hate

Marianne Morris

from Iran Documents

Solace Poem (after Parvin E'tesami)

Dear Friend,

        You started it. I am writing to you
        to explain about some of the feelings that I have. When
        they ask what I'm passionate about, and I
        sweep the ashtray.
        The pillow of a poetess is black with dust,
        she is a star of the firmament who tastes nothing
        but bitterness because her utterances are so sweet –
        but wait, that's not it.
        When I first said I was   going
        some of them said, 'Why would you
        want to
                ?'

            He is my love
          that solaces my heart
           in this dump

Qasida for Substance

1   A not-yet bed of grass, sunbleached, of wheat, colour-wise, legs
    take us there at liberty under question, see the spirit can move me

2   being two in a rhythm, hijacked like an ant instructed to climb
    eyes shut on the memories of things, women and their eyes, not

3   a good sign, and the phone, what was that, did it ring? Never mind
    how the year begins, how the ocean is alive, how its sudden heave is

4   breath swollen with seaweed fists. Movement belies depth and need,
    life at the edge of a final border, jurisdiction done, eyes sore with sun

5   eyes sore with how this must look, I can't face it. The fluorescent edge
    of fish under cellophane breathe cellular metaphors. Take time to admit

6   it was worked over, crushed under poorly-executed lists, bad resources
    admitting they want to vacuum the floor, to be lost in cake at night

7   to accumulate a layer of fat you'll hide in her sweatshirt. Before the
    months inside you there were other months, before the want of faith

8   translated to its breach, were other months. Newness is impossible.
    We made the rules ourselves, and can't think of anyone we want to be.

9   I can't look over there. I shield my face from clouds too ripped to
    indicate anything other than betrayal, forcing you to fail, wait

10   that will come later. The sky is a nightingale, cool until the heavens
    gently build a ladder up to touch blue, the entry fee is changeling,

11   insurmountable mount of myself. The governor of inwardness bars
    returning the call, wording the response, making it out into agency,

12   and I call it 'freedom', pellucid by force of slow intellect. We leave
    the edge for bed, a circle of grass pressed alone when I am alone.

13   Sun builds a canopy over lids to cradle lovers. Some living thing not
    human believes in love beyond the body of me or is it hopeless.

14   What choices do I have, what present leads to past, all timing burst
        fruition in the grass, all complication leading here: to talk of mourning

15   Ancestry denies my attempts, yet is on my side to provide examples
        : propagation, care, some other body's genius moved by spirit

16   what did Locke know. If I move you from a distance of 5,456 miles
        or zero feet pressed tight and invisibly joined and extremely moved

17   then that's god, Locke would say, if he knew. God in your mouth
        moves meekly to give me a name. Things are new in ways they have been

18   before. Each time on the curve after mild eucalyptus I get out and
        question the origin of luck is only good housekeeping you don't want

19   it. Fine-tuned pioneering, inherited aesthetics and hammer skills,
        if I am a body married to a spiritual mind, both finite machines

20   and indivisible, *codependent lovers*, neither one knowing where the
        pain or the need originates. Spent a long time jerking off.

21   Your face in digital swoop recalls the sky, the things of morning
        and of night killing wanderlust, bedtime batting, the voice cries evade,

22   sit and wait for the thing to become you, sit and wait for contractual
        disguise pending flight as intent to remain, no alarm but knowing heart

23   alarm that never shuts up. Everything you need is provided in the
        store, drugs and clothing scrummed by inaction passing stillness off

24   as freedom, good choices, information, the world borders on chaos
        everywhere but here. I flip coins against the sun mulling my mistakes,

25   fill my day with inherited wait, slap blueprint map over my face inert
        swaggering gas tank if I admit, at this late stage, that I want to learn

26   seems base in a day stretched out, the naked body mapping function
        I am a character, clown with no desires, perhaps food has affected

27   my desires. Perhaps speech implodes interrogation and desires are
        intimate things unhampered inside, but my mouth falls, and my feet lock

28   into running, can do nothing except run. Fake this ad pile that on,
laughing at the thing in your eyes, laugh at loving from a series

29   of ambivalent concerns. What do I want? Noise, devotion, even here
America spreads its thing and lines the London street, light drowned

30   in the pale clout of traffic, flattening the palette of pavement I dream
to, sirens incant beneath email his lack of things to lose. So many

31   shocking pretensions you grab at slipping away in a ding-dong state
discuss habits, functional nick-nacks, speech underwater, take notes

32   is what I do, not breaking past the cushioning damp of fear, not my own
but those that love me fear improbable things. I am the opposite of danger

33   but I fear being impolite. On which so much silence is at stake, mistake
my animation for something more, beneath a veneer people fucking move

34   in and out of sync with their lives. Comfort myself with invisible lines,
how the sounds move the mouth, and duly expect the shift to fall out

35   the way it always does. Next to me they speak, I long to join them,
past my life and lines deciding. This thing, this character, this way.

36   Stop being so fucking nice. Another mask
I intend to don, mask of myself. Keep my voice down, don, don't

37   smile so much. Want so much to be different, fuck loving what
you are. Yes stop putting Ehud Olmert at ease. *Everyone* is nice

38   when they relax before the fire. If money is going to be spent then
why not hack hungover screed, place bets instead, bet this:

39   that the sum total will amount to a life lived in thought, and not
the pithy moments of immediacy, present tense a last gasp that goes

40   tumultuously down the street, paved insemination with a baster in
my thought that drove me, absent trajectory, how much louder I

41   would sing if it was blood in me that did it, and not because of The
Guardian, or for any reason other than the propeller, stiff in my gut,

42   sides split time holed up sex the only possibility. Can you live with
        me, I ask myself as I'm getting older now, my face is lined

43   with abstinence and the sum total of my days in page form, stripped
        down to evenings spent coughing into the void, gazing blankly

44   as a lover flounders amongst the vibrant gazing others.
        Prey.

45   Crux of speed that melted your head, no edge, how do you feel
        about this: all of the lined pathways have already been walked

46   only moments before, and by groups with dogs, and they barked
        at them for obedience, and the dogs didn't bark back. On this

47   painful solitude I cast a series of friendly smiles, by the end of
        it my face is sore. Politeness written into the flightpath. I can't gain

48   access to any plurality, I want to know how I can be different, my
        face sagging in the mirror as I'm getting older now, and wanting

49   hampering with blissful weight, not time fetishizing distant pain,
        try to reach the hurting things around me, and know not *seems*.

from The On All Said Things Moratorium

Compose Message

make it speak, hit it
speech

> fall to caress lovingly a dead
> poetry burst its shell & weeps life out

consider the weightless aspect
life in stringy sky & clouds green on faces is a photograph
but a severed also moment I crave

> anxious made

wait until explosions disperse, as if no one were around well but
there you are, I can't

> how I mean it is the final surge
>
> > but that exactly unends.

ii.

– if that girl, passing on her mobile phone, is
our mistrusting mistress, time,
and if she looks at me whilst passing
> I am involved in the wild smile –

iii.

sad, slow exercise, poor mechanic,
off on holes with a broken vehicle,
> tinkering at things

like grief & cold
needs to do this only, it tugs at he
> blinks back the price in

eyes blood, & dead, & urging now towards the final rest of
sudden silence, unexpected, cannot prevent it now

iv.

oceans of days run out to become other trees,
like music, or water in the bath,
                  forged calm shudders on a daft excuse
& an uncontrollable urge to control
                  & thus remain
glistening on the cusp of an actual shine on it,
           dust polish
                  coping wild to keep that held memory,
                  where you hold
sticks, or finger a vine,
                  disaster of the past, kneading definite memory
                  as something more suitable to this moment
which is cast out,
              vines, cast stomped grape through
              that wringer, your gorgeous split
              throat now opening,
              admitting the sour taste you wait for
constantly, open to suggestion.
              stop, break it. does how it spill then
              mean a thing; when catching up to a point
              in time most wanted for,
                  most caressed & lulled at distance
                  into
being a self desperate wishes. no, stop.
              gathers it in her arms, stooping gathers.
              the poison bush all blossomed & berried
              goes to sit in,
                  picking lyric apart. most
                  natural of exercises,
the sad mechanic picks him up, & a pen,
              forging with sense,
              sense
                  into a place that rules
                  it's in your blood now carousing
merry great abundance, grow & get & better &
                  vitiate, & how
prenuptial, & avoid
                  disturbing, & it's, &
kill a, enervate, make a
      distribution,
                  without hope is hopeless, that's good,

turn the disaster to a better thing,
      though the pain in me lower
      than is in me needed,
          budding, disproves this theory.
mostly felt in the heart, its own
        rhythm collapsing. in a last,
        moment, lasting
               divided brackets into time.
culling the dainty lyric with a
        flick of the disjoint
        wrist, admit
              collisions & peruse them.
fall to your
        look to your
              instructed bashes out
eyes & all instruments,
        all records of this remove
            to what happened
when your world was nothing but its axis
        of wild
            disturbed words,
all of which cling to nothing, I will say,
        how does it go,
        in your bed at
            morning escaping vicious
words that have racked the skull taunting so
        long ago as to nearly come
        mocking up the
            explains the
this; I see where you are from this protracted
        filth of action, & I urge
          you get your
free urge,
      get free of if they are to be that
    sole   hope
           they must mean what
they must mean all
        that you are
          my love,
             I tell you so.

Erín Moure

from O Cidadán

To intersect a word: citizen. To find out what could intend/distend it, today. *O cidadán.* A word we recognize though we know not its language. It can't be found in French, Spanish, Portuguese dictionaries. It seems inflected "masculine." And, as such, it has a feminine supplement. Yet if I said "a cidadá" I would only be speaking of 52% of the world, and it's the remainder that inflects the generic, the *cidadán*. How can a woman then inhabit the general (visibly and semantically skewing it)? How can she speak from the generic at all, without vanishing behind its screen of transcendent value? In this book, I decided, I will step into it just by a move in discourse. I, a woman: o cidadán. As if "citizen" in our time can only be dislodged when spoken from a "minor" tongue, one historically persistent despite external and internal pressures, and by a woman who bears – as lesbian in a civic frame – a *policed sexuality*. Unha cidadán: a semantic pandemonium. If a name's force or power is "a *historicity* ... a sedimentation, a repetition that congeals," (Butler) can the name be reinvested or infested, fenestrated ... set in motion again? Unmoored? Her semblance? Upsetting the structure/stricture even momentarily. *To en(in)dure, perdure.*

To move the force in any language, create a slippage, even for a moment ... to decentre the "thing," unmask the relation...

document2 (inaugural)

As if we are that dichogamous flower, each of us. Nancy locates the resistances of sense as a "touching on the confines of the world." How to write the sense of the world? Our cared selves a product always of migrations or emigrative qualities, out of, a surge within a name burst open like a pod of light in which we see Vigo or Londres, the small path along the wall behind which are rows of vines. An *existentiale* of worldliness, says Nancy: resistance to the closure of worlds within the world.

O cidadán a seal or bond with this world, nothing to do with country or origin. The cidadán stands in time as the person stands in space, liquid edge before or beyond the other she craves, the she she craves also a she, and this is space that opens time,
> it is a space
> where time tumbles backwards, *brings a* future *into* presence

A public space is where we are both signs, O Claire. Our epochal inclination.

                   (Where "the court of agriculture is the border of grace," "shouting eliminates governors.")

proclitic enclitic diaeresis dias technē

Georgette

Dignified is a heartsong here
Harsh traverse of the unknown

"Better to go down dignified"
Ekes out
constant

What gives in us, or won't give
(her smile seen once in the Red Café)

Turns sparkless
Into sparklers

One "s" less
One "r" more, Georgette

———

The new wall we built that year
where the house side had been torn out

Grammar we called in

like a bet on narrative

———

Now I am the only one who hasn't yet gone in;
and I have these sentences

(fissures in the hand)

Second Catalogue of the Substitution of Harms*

		√	

harm	harm	harm	harm	harm
———	———	√	———	———
forms	term	devices	units	count

harm	harm	harm	harm	harm
———	———	———	———	√
world	bath	abs	kid	advised

harm	harm	harm	harm	harm
———	———	———	———	———
arm	mayors	pain	nother	comedies

harm
———
influenced

                    fractions
* in the form of ~~functions~~

document4 (weights)

"The units of weight" and their "frank" exchange. To say "the resistance to the unacceptable [unha cidadán, for example] itself ought to proceed from another sense," invokes submission/domination as a frank meeting of two potentates, in a cut edge of undecidability, for submission's band turns (a möbius)

and compels,
invites to, insists on being met, calls forth "want" urgency in the other and fond display or concoctability of this urgency as "form"

"amid"

To construct the self is to be amid (necessitate) (prior?) civic space
or coil

Horticulture in a pear   her constraint is "pearls" to preen
hollow way
A further price to whey anatomy whose curl of light

There was an extension after what we heard
Guess a prologue   an immense chorale

(who signed this)

(are awakened)

invertebrate inveterate fallacy accuse

Fourth Catalogue of the Underwater Locker of Thieved Harms

Did harms' encyclical hold us in?
We compelled such harms, they said, like *bruxas*.

Mark's surface marked; mark
being where script endures

Fearless ambiguities in the clause.
A "wet" "fromage"

What I wrote in you, written against
all harm, and you the wettening surface
I declare upon
not advisedly but with splendours

and drapery; Velásquez risen from a Spanish tomb
to represent your dress

against the wet "frond" risen of that drapery
I raise above your knee

when I ask of you to lease caress
squatting upon my hand's murmur

or insistenence a trail
to become

unheld by that confine or boundary

(Egress me here)

(or ease)

(this frank equivalence)

Georgette

What starts as a doubt
within the membrane of a fissure
within the unspeakable apparatus
of the membrane
can become a woman
Yesterday

years before us

A wit's world for example
a level used to measure
the accuracy of a wall's construct
our corporeal wall or construct
device used for imperative projection
before the cornucopic ectopy
the simultaneous legacy or legislative
quality

Years later   a body   does this

illustrate
To illustrate

document5 (dehiscence' tiny cape)

Cixous reads Clarice Lispector's *Paixão* as *aproximação* – approach or approximation – and it is political: the "between-us" which we must touch with care. Here, too, Nancy: "The word *world* has no unity of sense other than this one: a world is always a differential articulation of singularities that make sense in articulating themselves,

along the edges of their articulation..."

What if we all craved a poetic document, exquisitely worked each word a lattice of ingenuity? I don't believe this. To make sense is perhaps, as I read, to be susceptible to indication (not *definition*). If I were the tiny cape, you were your entries below another highway in the year of oxidation. What is allowable beyond a certain measure. Contiguous without absorption. As if to show you what I am wearing:

```
a b c d e f g h i j k l
m n o p q r s t u v w
x y z
```

———— ———— ———— ————

her article to touch or not her article.

my lips miss "kindred"

Zinc bar on the rue de Rennes (Au Vieux Colombier)

Salt. Amorousness. A cliff or cleft, or wind.

Boundary or knee. Rain

<98.11.12/Paris>

I was destroying the horizon. So wooden a tradition – pain – was functioning: they who had requested it rose to compete. Because that board occupies those landscapes' fevers, a blood life is a promise. To crash repairs this, but Europe is a lie between the degree and the medicine, test or label. Why were you voting? Why had these struggles mattered? The vulgar vestibule between these distances and the range (your talent) is steam. How I have existed? Whom can't the chair of soil stop? Because to extend laughs, the celebrating notion above the guard is some battery of underdogs except shame. Sequences are shapes. Tapes had talked. Don't events want intervals? I have embellished the row of error, the hope of folklore, the viburnum, the possible talent, the design of wonder. My emblem should stop.

> misquoted from Livy,
> *History of Rome*

Jennifer Moxley

from The Line

THE LINE

True faith does not need the state to enforce it. It makes neither hope, nor a shroud. You will walk out of the visible and learn to accept the darkness. You will find the line. It extends backwards eternally into the past and forward into the future. The utterance cup, the gentle metric, old words new mind lost time and loves. You sensed it all along, but gaining the knowledge was hopelessly muddled by the inherent drive to author new life. Now cut the spittle line spun into reason and enter the grave alone.

In other words, write. Find time in words. Replace yourself cell by letter, let being be the alphabetic equation, immortality stay the name.

MYSTICAL UNION

Infused with an early century's fatigue you dream you can never wake up. Your thought, a small dot on the horizon, is overtaken by traffic. Huge semis whiz by issuing noxious black smoke. Are they pushing the world's cheap goods onto the local market? Everything's plastic and bright. Mimics of vulgar joy, the people refuse their misery. In between moments of stupor they awkwardly waddle forward. Are they to blame?

You dream the end of life has been forsaken by a world in ruins. Someone performs an amputation to tie the resources up. Your children are threatened not by a system but by a single unethical man. The air shimmers. You step off the curb into nothingness where the line offers itself to your hands. Grab hold or fall. Happy in the thought you might never recover you consign your trust to this flimsy thread that nobody else can see.

THE ENDLESS CONSCRIPTION

The chaperone of brittle egos, with her porous empathy cage of a body, lives like an automaton among living beings. Even after the last granules of dirt have settled on her charges, the heavy shovel has been tossed away, and the rain has finally stopped falling, she is not safe. Somehow the famished ghouls always rise again. Buried by their apathy years ago, she knows how they feel. Moldering and useless beings, their overweening crisp egos wander the hallways of her cavernous guilt. "Shhh" they gesture with their sexless fingers, "we only want you to listen."

THE PERIODIC TABLE

She was wearing a dress that looked like a book but actually was a baby. All of the letters were on her back to make room for her bulging stomach. I climbed through many foreign backyards in search of my bedroom window. I lived on Ire Street off of Sport in room one hundred and ten. The mailbox was filled with paychecks or grade sheets, I couldn't tell the difference. Is this my name or isn't it? Pink, yellow, and white, a temporary carbon-based witness.

I sleep with approximately 14,000 days sitting on my chest. A slow hour many years old pushes aside yesterday's appetites and enters as a whisper through an unmuffled ear: "remember me, remember me, remember me!" And so the incantation continues until I open my eyes to find that I am changed into a patient on a table. Wait, it's not me, it's my mother. Men are taking her out on a stretcher. Oh no. blood, blood, everywhere!

THE LOST BIRD

Every time I held out my finger he flew to me and rested there. He was a tiny Indigo Bunting whose wings beat a furious pace. Then one day I had to go away. My trip began down a long stairway that led into a tunnel. I held my finger above my head and the bird came to me, but when I began to descend, he fluttered his wings and remained in the air. I tried to trap him in my cupped hands but whenever I did I felt guilty. I wanted him to come willingly.

RUN THROUGH

Here's to a rhythm that follows the ear. Or rather, here's to you, heavy genealogy, you've been making me hungry for years. Mimesis was your meal ticket. The bounty went right through you when it should have become a door. A door to where? To some place beyond these endless deserts of shoddy salvation.

The legacy of your discomfort with loss and retention has made me the victim of my digestion. It's all a matter of perspective, and I am, as the vehicle of these violent processes, completely ignorant of how they work. I must guess based on non-mechanical evidence and a total integration of the senses. They shall become one and none. Then the line inside my belly will show itself to my mind as it passes the boundary of my body's calendar into an infinity of days. Though this hook-up may pain me, I suspect it necessary.

THE MATTRESS RAFT

Leaving the bird behind I went on my journey. I found my brother and an old friend I hadn't spoken to in years. They were in a room at the bottom of a perfectly groomed sand dune. The incline was very steep. At the top was a mattress cliff which looked like solid matter. If only I could reach it! My friend was already there. She extended her arm down. I grabbed it with one hand and with the other I grabbed the edge of the fabric. My feet fruitlessly pedaled the promontory of salt-like sand, but finally, finally, I made it up to the firm white plane of ticking. Now only my brother remained. He did an aerial somersault into the cliff and then lay stiff and lifeless. I panicked and tried to call for help but my fingers were totally useless. In my anger I started to cry. What an idiot! Why did he choose inevitable defeat by picking the fancy solution?

THE END

Cock-sure of the end the Saint chose instead to think about the beginning. You know nothing of either. Of course, there are legends. At both your birth and her death your concerned mother pushed you away because she was ill. Within these parentheses you probe the mysteries. Will you be punished? Probably.

For years you have been seeking an alternative company in the compressed life-force of entropic matter, but today you are suspicious of its seductions: touch me, shape me, hold me it says, but it is never easy to do so. These various forms of material resistance have charmed away over half of your life. Not to worry, once you are gone there won't be anyone to interpret the meaning of the things you have loved.

THE INTERRUPTION

Half-way to the poetical mind, defenses, like worldly trappings as you enter the Great Below, laid aside one by one, the line just coming into view, you are called back home to play gracious hostess to the endless string of scribblers. Serious or unserious, appreciative or not, they are helpless in these woods. Empathy! Kindness! Where are they? Lost like light-pink baby socks with soiled lace trim by the side of the road. In their place an obliterative drive to lose self-consciousness in linguistic equations. If it weren't for the endless conscription of the socially conditioned female this illegal transaction of souls could take place while the impossible Ego kept watch. Then when you were called back it would be with your mouth shut and through the gate of false dreams.

POSSESSED

At dinner you accuse your lover of gross inattention to detail. You begin impassioned then turn resentful. He will have none of it. "Don't yell at *me*," he coolly says. As the candlelight blears with enraged disbelief an albatross lifts you by the scruff of the neck and pulls you magically through the roof. "Have you forgotten how to fly?" it asks in an exasperated tone. "That life may be fixed, but you are still free." "Don't you remember the middle room lessons? Fragile mammals prove bad compasses – use the horizon instead."

from Imagination Verses

THE WINGÈD WORDS

What are these wingèd words
that have escaped the barrier
of your teeth?
    Nothing doing,
nor my fault the Ford
won't start and so
    as walked across
you become land,
    bedded be my wilderness
    bookish my landscape and sea
    a bridgeless head tease.
Would you deign me everyday
if nearly to you
I were to say: "hey,"
    would you find me
contemporary
if Aristide stood for options
betoken of banks on which
no pronominal carrier
can stand
or gaze upon singers sweetly singing? O Ramona...
    my ocean is sold
    my ships of steel
    and all my nuclear submarines have drifted.

A man on the corner
begs experience
as moments pass   into the panhandler.
Were we the land's
before we were landed?   And then suddenly
things meant homelessness,
    alas my youth disbanded
    asleep in the automatic
    teller machine booth
while all the while
you stepped up to carpet
and a brand new skin product,

as sadly I am now comforted
by leather.   *brick upon brick...*
If Aristotle stood for options well
                    brick upon brick...
a skin head with a leadpipe
in the conservatory,
                    brick upon broken
neck, thanks to my skin
it only happens
in my shipwrecked sleep.

What are these wingèd words
that have escaped the barrier
of my teeth?
               Nothing doing.
an evasive act
as when the lights go up
and you no longer like
licking me and the thing
becomes thoughtlessness,
                    lick upon lick
engineered, it's
autocratic eroticism, a person
to person phone call
to my personal she-history whip.
    Whose sovereignty?
    surrounded by working
    papers and men my markings
a downtown trench
circled by suburbs and upwards
of one hundred stories of sky.
It could even become our own arms race.

THOUGH CROWDED

I am not thinking of you
always, in separation our time
is queer requirement, the
impossible revelation
of a moment alone, or the
pale counting of debts.
Alone in thought my mind
now falters, accomplishments
are my heavy buildings reached,
they mark the jeopardy
of savings, must I think
of everything as saved,
the daylight, all the world
of time I want you in shall
pass ungathered. Will you
insist for love my life
must make effective changes,
while throughout this
makeshift home the rooms
are filled with savings,
photographs and books
acquired as if my very life
on them depended.
Tonight I saw the moon
in the faint sky of Providence
and I was moved no deeper
for the distance. You must
know what you've done
to my ambition.

Redell Olsen

from Punk Faun: A Bar Rock Pastel

from the capitals of every pilaster
a strange music of wild instruments
scene divided into two parts from the roof to the floor
the consorts both sound again
as one amazed speaks
pages return toward the scene
while this cloud was vanishing the wood being the under-part of the scene
was insensibly changed
in place thereof appeared four of silver
the first order consists of all gold, set with rubies, sapphires, emeralds, opals
and such like
the capitals were composed and of new invention
over this was a bastard order with cartouches reversed
the upper part rich and full of ornament
full song supported now by clouds
their arms converted into scrolls
under their waists a foliage and other carvings
bore up an architrave from which was raised a light covering arched
interwoven with branches through which the sky beyond was seen
their habits were mixed between ancient and modern
shoulders trimmed with knots of pure silver
in the upper parts where any earth could fasten were some strange forms
so high as the top pierced the clouds
the chorus of the beloved people came forth
led by Concord and the Good Genius of Great Britain
their habits being various

they go up to the state and sing

opening as a curtain of artificial sea flows itself abroad tinned aisles

sails on pop soup storm blankets thrown to arms with polymer smile

their cults were spoken of wherever there were cans

fleet of foot calorific numerologists compare motives in daily fix-up

in jest hieroglyphics Elvis Liz Marilyn condensed in mute packaging

sky – only not as recess – walking as on flats of – colour deployed

then across – whole cylinders attract – float – arms – becoming

branches – surprise lack – an admission of a reached ledge

        shoulders sprout – whole lift – trees or sky in

        retreat – shapes made river – pencil clouds

        marked – play lines at bodies – float weight

        arms branch – above clasp – breeze takes reach

        of lead –

gildings owed custom branded labels for bottled water all covered camera

free speech by numbers in interests of a fair gamble and easy wipe thrones

their cults were spoken of wherever there were ads

lifted from a birds eye view frozen moons chicken winged charioteers free

range fans inscribed names merged at chocolate fountain of domestic lip

skin barks against sky – pains waking – static no longer – goes

ploy of figuring – tackle to bring down – stats of limbs in flight cannot

hold so gives – twig tress – entwining legs – ledge in inked

> sky – the balletic hop – where the weight is clasp
>
> to arms – call becoming out as branch graze
>
> pixel beyond skirts – cursor at cupid click – insert
>
> pale for back – lines equal horizons – the ledge
>
> as a screen

demographics of personalised pop-ups gone global in the run up

to requisite blankness bespoke mailers who do the epistolary lick

their cuts were spoken of wherever there were candies

service splendours joined forever in the decoration of a house price

or going public in the lobby with a shared plaque above the bench

yellow is for distance – sky only backs out – a flat wept in area

a ballet clasp over one – an arm wrench – the weight is hurt

weight is blue or is a dress – cannot hold lives – edge tears

ledgewise to under

> pink specs for human – gold for fur – sky clog
>
> varnish – blue distains back – dress of bunching
>
> an admission marks – eyes down – branch harms
>
> figures certain in drapery – lodge hold

of ceilings

two breathe clouds across the sky to one another

being scarred by birds they stand on wavy air

push on neighbouring particles to make tunes I

permanently bound into the stuff of naked walls

slaked lime paste and coarse marble on canapés

between points of compression the china bones

as see through this longitudinal nicety gasps up

tempo as do I I do resounds over shelves rusty

in casting shapely hearts or how the head holds

a flood marker gauges stubborn wet lime marked

in place of face grinds pigment for speaking out

of rheuming it through violently spun air blubbers

a funnel for listening with what cannot be fanfare

stronger for liquid intake concrete quibbles stick

but in itself does not vibrate stocks of the same

if all surfaces are magnets then we might travel

cheaply outside to find ourselves encrusted at

the navel with the body of a man or the torso of

a horse and buy it up in expectation of the pain

in kick that is deployed as a mammal might be

in enemy waters where even dolphins have teeth

pulling away fast from what look like shells AWOL

or just meeting up with the other local marine life

to search for patterns at every nth click tears

past Standard Gas Stations gestations in series

painted in black and orange L'AMOUR or L=I=S=P

spelled out in ribbons rime can be thick enough

to resemble shades enchanted for repel of damage

a slide show primer (on behalf of the warden)

This is of a chord sprinkled thicket

This is of a diagram which proves it

This is of a footnote that explains what pancakes are

This is of a perpetual fear of those on the outside whose job it is to grid the internals

This is of a pure flank

This is of a shape that is not always an innocent container

This is of a tufted slumber

This is of an abstract thing or it might be a nipple

This is of an ear as it would be seen inflating from inside the body

This is of artificial breath

This is of a caudal appendage or so-called tethered form

This is of imported seedless gapes

This is of not just human

This is of nothings purring

This is of nylon and how it suspends many small things that would otherwise be falling

This is of one laughing as an expression of foolishness

This is of one laughing who does not appear to be expressing anything

This is of one of those funny pink things Eva Hesse made before she went grey

This is of one rollerblading through an airport

This is of one that is like some string coiled up

This is of one weeping as an expression of ecstasy

This is of one weeping who does not appear to be expressing anything

This is of one which is quite like the sign nearby that says not to

This is of one which might have been used as a squeaker for a small dog

This is of signals from a kept live and natural wild wild

This is of some ears with pointed ends

This is of some safety pins which were used to keep it together

This is of some string coiled up

This is of some verbal wallpaper as was vetoed by the warden

This is of the fur in transit and still breathing

This is of the heart of the timid

This is of the increased through the perforation and damage

This is of the long yellow ropes that were used

This is of the other side of the scaffolding as Clovis saw it

This is of the place where it was found to be punctured

This is of the same consistency as the resin that clogged the interior and made
       it difficult to say anything

This is of the she-wolf suckling

This is of the taxi driver with paws or maybe they were just gloves

This is of the way the joke was found face down in a lay-by past caring

This is of tresses knotted in horns

This is of use within properly prescribed limits

Holly Pester

Grills

Ah knew ma grandma was different
by the way she bent
over to pick up dust instead af
hoover

what are we bears
to do with paper
if ah drew an animal ah drew its beak and snow grills
then ah can imagine its dashboard
it moved

tha look ah me
because
tha love me ma sun
and tha know ma ahdiosyncrasies

ah have low confidence in ma dad
a sea bare farer he sleeps
with bares
he ha real-live insects

all over tha floor
his hoover broke
he ha no confidence

it's ahdiocy
Ma mum cleans insects off har wall
no she doesn't but she should
ahh she's in debt
thar is strength in numbers

ah am mooning
what if ma mother's bear came home through the hole
ma brothar kicked when we teased him for his ahhguitar
ma parents ah dun kitty
ar grandparents got down in the dumps
thar lost their money in snow grills and bare fists
if ah'm not sick into pottery
who will

Ma parents are snow grills
ah man makes his rake sing
spent all his tin on woman drinking gin
What doesn't tha man want?

every year thar is a sale in Essex and so goes ma ahdiom

ah forget why women drank gin
or sewed up pillows
ah diagram for a new desk is a level of improvement and optimism and pottery
ah am comfortable with

What ma grandma knew was
bare fits
and very very very easy chinese food
ah ahah
she knew har husband was
a grill
and had arms
ah am optimistic that
ma grandad was ah very good artist

(The squid woke up when he heard his name and rose from where he was lying on the riverbank. The squid was a maker, he cleared his throat and he raised his voice.)

The Squid's Poem, 'To Draw a Blank'

Warm-up

Some thing some thing some thing mo ney some wine
Some thing some thing some thing mo ney some loose change
Man loose man loose man loose ly park
Re cord re cord re cord of my tu dor
Fi far me draw me pick le far le far
With cold fi hands twis twine mi wane a ha
And tear it my hi ding un der de neath
A dress E liz a beth that can y' see
A pear ring like a bear of bark.
In bags I found a blank et sheet it was'a bot big piece
It's there it's there it's here
Mad pieces I have fallen to pieces

In thee beginning Queen Elizabeth
A made the lottery, all so, the floor.
And Queen Elizabeth said, yar my bank, yar
Queen Elizabeth ditty that, for usall
He said, bad luck him who lost thee lott'ree
happy me Pieces mee lotta mary.
Be less you! Duh Mister le Queen Eliz
Abeth, I want numbers of swans of swans
of swans of swam solar panel and a tart
I know not how to thank enough, my Queen
Elzzy beth. When I do walk over too
to you I just want to behold the blank
But you to me give blankets, covers!
I know not how to thank nough, mister
le Queen Elizabut! When I am walk
king ova to it I just want to pick
numbers But you give numb burroughs
I know not how to thank you nuff, mister,
my Queen Elizabeth. When I am walk
king through to you I just want simple swans
But you me give in French a swanary
Her Majesty's Deputy Master for
the Swans', was there ever such a Treash zurer
of Lottery in grave Surrey. The Lost

lee Manuscript is dull. A unique archive
of More-Money. My family who fart
for centuries with more money to dove
in rows big beautiful Tudor manors
big house is Loseley Park. The manuscript
contains unique records of my Tudor life
Stuart is Queen England with More money
Describe the lottery re for me dear
Red ball red bell red ball a hound a fag
Like your leg glows the swan, blossoms
Le calmly calm as Queen England is poor
Rest hope of spring. My heart follows y'hou,
it likes your beer voice and it leaps like numbers,
it shouts me your name, Stuart-the-Blank
The eve venning did float on great finance,
Com forted by a hair that was found here
carry into the light of pencilbeams
and hold next to my big fig head
Im full with hope and more money than you
so Might I try the pot William sir
he found some spare money and numer rous
other big boxes full of sacks of sand
As my real small arse falls from my trousers
it does remind me of a bank of yours
It's quiet, so I listen for the last
Little jingle of pay tuday. My hot
fat foot it leaps to my shu shoes. I wait
in moonlight for a secret gas so we
might try gamble as one, fat foot to foot,
in search of the mag nif fi cient, in search
of the mystical balls of rent. THANK YOU

And so said the squid, and he was a squid of rank.

BUDDUHOLLYONMYANSWERMACHINE

Peggy S_
Peggy S_
Peggy S_
Pretty pretty ptty petty pty pty pty

      P
        eggy Sue
Hu-ho hu-ho
<u>Peggy</u> ↓   my ↑
c
  - - -
Peggy ↓   my.↑

        PEG ↠↠↠↠↠
Creep creep creep creep creep   eeeeeEGG

HU – hue hu -hue hu-hue hue hue

↓with alove ↓so so with alove ↓see so alove so ↓with so sea sway alove sew
say rare and
true↑ slip
patchy↑
my
 p eggy ↠
Su – he – hoo he- hoo B! he – hoo B! he- hoo-he-hoo-hoo
He-hoo- He-hooo he-hoo hoop

hoop
smash
hoop
smash
hoop
CRAB
       Peggy – peggy – peggy – peggy – peggy – peggy – peggy – peggy – peggy
<u>Pegg</u>
y↓   Sew

say crab - bee‹

MY ↑   crab ↓

Crab ↓- bee ↑
My ↑
crab ↓ ring
Ring ring?

My clunk. Clunk clunk
My clunk
My heart clunk
My clunking heart clunk
My ↑ Heart ↑ Yearns ↑
my ↑ heart ↑ yearns ↑
my ↑ heart ↑ yearns ↑
my ↑ heart ↑ yearns ↑
my ↑ heart ↑ yearns ↑
my ↑ heart ↑ yearns ↑
My shivering heart
my heart shivering
my shiver
shivering

Sticky-sticky-sticky-sticky-sticky- sticky-sticky-sticky-sticky- sticky-sticky-sticky

Peggy Sue
Peggy flew
Peggy soak

A – ho Achy ↑
My Achy-su-hu—hoo

Back
back
back
back gate

Wella left ja girl ----- HAIR
Wella left ja hair hair girl
Peggy Hair
Peggy hair hair
Peggy
who

Who-hoo-who-whoo-wh-hoo-hoo Who? Peggy ↑
Peggy sleeps ↑
Peggy ↑
hoo-who
I luft you ↑ Paid to sit ↑
Peggy ↓ paid to chew ↑
I luft chew ↑
painful shit
plummy ↓
witha lump
So ↑ rare ↑ and ↑ true ↑
With alove so rarey true
So rare it flew
Rarey ↓
Weed their love solar lunchroom
Week their love cellular room
Weed their love slowly a room
Hairy
So rare it's tru.e
Weedy

Oh Peggy ↓
My Peggy spewed

Well when I love you go in whenever you can / malevolently cool / and well
now because I want to pay you soon / well I love you turn one she wants to pay
me spew / well I love you turn one she wants to see me pay / well I love you
turn one she paid to see me sew

Anna want chu Peggy Seed.
With a lump too rare to sew

I uv you ↑ **Pe**ggy spew
              Peggy speed
              Peggy rock
Peggy shot

  Pretty

              pitty
              pitty
                petite
          pity

pretty
>> **Pe**ggy Stroke ↑
>> **Pe**pper shake ↑

Pete Postlethwaite
Ponchos Pilot
Polygon
Planet Earth
Pythagoras
Please please me
Particle accelerator
Proboscis
Puffin eggs

>> **Pa**y me now ↑

Pay me now ↑
Pay me now ↑

Puffin eggs

Peggy billowed and spewed
Pillow begged
Pillow begging and sewing
Pillow begg
Peggy shook

Vanessa Place

Forgiveness

The detective introduces himself; says he wants to talk about
what happened with appellant's nephew.

The detective says that when men do something wrong, they
ask for forgiveness; appellant asks for forgiveness.

Appellant asks if the judge could send him to Mexico: he's
thinking about his kids.

He says he'll never come back. He doesn't understand his
body, asks for forgiveness, asks it for his kids

She says he was thinking about killing her; he says he doesn't want to keep fighting with her. He asks her whether she loves him anymore. She says she does not. She asks him to admit what he did to her. He says it was a mistake and asks for her forgiveness. She wants him to apologize, he says he told her mother that he was sorry.

Appellant says he would have liked to face Celeste and ask for forgiveness.

Elena asks if appellant is sorry, he says he is "very, very, very sorry" but doesn't want to tell anyone.

Appellant says he's really sorry for everything, he didn't take care of business right and is stupid.

Mitchell asks what appellant would say to Blakee in fifteen years' time; appellant says she's sorry for "hurting you," and that she "loves you so much." She's sorry for lying and says what she did was stupid.

Appellant also provided a written statement which said that he requested Josefina and Ynez's forgiveness with all his heart.

Appellant's letter said that he had been told she felt bad because he never said sorry to her. He asks her to forgive him, and to tell her mother to forgive him. He writes that it was not his intention to hurt Tamara and never thought it would make her feel bad. He says he loves her very much. He writes to his partner that he loves her and asks her to forgive him. He says he loves all of them with all his heart. There is a smiley face drawn at the end of the letter with a balloon coming from the smiley face saying, "Sweetie, I love you Dull Say." After the signature, he wrote that he hoped they would forgive him.

Appellant asks for forgiveness. He regrets what he has done.
The detective asks appellant if he wants to write that;
appellant says he does not know how to write.

She did not appear at a prior trial: the November 8th
letter stated that she missed her father, had forgiven him, and did
not want him to go to prison.

Sophie Robinson

from The Institute Of Our Love In Disrepair

She! The Revolution Rooms

bathroom

Water-landscaped chamber, flat-roofed –
A set of matching units to be fitted.
"this is the good sun, the necessary
to look sun." You wanted & you faded there:
She could see the twilight dilating in
his eyes, feel his economics coming on

"What you wanted you took: my closed-off
remembering, your superstructure,
terry-cloth inches several & feathers
torn & bruised from sullen arms – a mood of
murder, corporeal cold – slow, slow, my
destination, humming, slow, slow—

We meet in the mirror & in brief panties
of breath we touch each other lightly &
feel sick, awake." Prune-faced, pimpled, she puffs
her body out as wall to wall canvas
of stretched skin, so early, so slipped & those
sauces drool down hard, down chins, jawlines.

Gossip in the morning, raised & splayed
spray recoiling from her, no wish to sluice –
"Mine's an oozing red," a sweetheart, a
perpetual happening in the bowl
beside herself & softly she is not
a boy. Her better fingers dream of dressing.

Angular muttering squeezed between
soapy thighs & this room resists her, a
porcelain imprint as gift on her throbbing
personality. *"Clutch me clean, no crime, no crime..."*
A simple pill, a place to cup herself inside –
Whose insides? Whose production? Whose crime?

"This is the good dark, the night-light dark." Slippered
whispers, sleazy little simpatico hours,
moisture-beaded that private signal, adored.
eggs, semi-draped | beauty, half-dissembled
lavatory yellow, extra-lemon
a little fatter, flush – slow destiny.

We flinched again – you'll clear the glob – legs of blood,
of satin stocking under plaintive offspring
percolating in hose, tight, tighter still
to whack me on the carriageway then nurse
my wounds – the balconied, the abnormal,
the slow destination, humming, humming.

*"Those awful sisters are the athlete of
my hurt,"* the rigid door, the relentless
ooze of summer, finding your intimate you,
your singlehanded paperback, knees rising,
head sinking down into the gray nausea pool,
rib's noise engaged to crack, to gag & hum.

This is water worth pressing. *"All my wounds
are in the front. My tear, my maxi-
opportunity, nouveaux riches, shuffled-up
deity, incantations at regular
o'clock."* Cologne, toothpaste, leathery jilt
against the cheeks of quick & boring men.

Mixed drinks, melodramatic moments –
She, a non-fiction touch-machine
Zigzagged animals, roller curls
The uncomfortable significance
of her blondness as heady pollen
to be eaten now & seen again later.

Chin shadows curve the day away,
Unhook her with scissors: bathroom exile.
Thrust, sunny thrust, fisherman's snag,
The comparative horror of a slipped rug
Toweling skywards, splashing ochre
Of left behind flesh up walls as wet paper.

She is naked, screaming, this is not a
metaphor. To habituate or
symbolize this thought is nothing less.
You think of bathrooms as transitory
places, but people can die there, humming,
dark sun, slow destination, humming.

She! Retro Love Songs

*

Do you in all my emptiness feel me
felt like dollies? I wish now to tie my
self inside your strange & static chest. Coins
astonish me, sitting yellowish and
relenting as ornaments worn around
your neck. You have the most benevolent
hips this side of god. I would eat the pole
which holds your constellation steady in
a second, wolfishly.

*

Every subtle jibe is a flint from the core
fundamental secrecy is fundamentally yours
we front our phony accumulations as back
but you have a crosser hunger to attend to.

If this is the luggage of love then I'm gone.
Widen your blinders for this sneak, our town
about as reassuring as a hammer at dusk at
the edge of twilight.   Parked glass globs us.

*

the portal of personal misery is located right of
an act which debases women.
The line of your identification
leads you to it.

Here is the living underside
of hushed obstacles.

Toward her, a cantata of grace (part one: suture)

If I were you and you were me I would
turn and turn again, move my arms from left
to right, I would large I would small I would
seek out all the danger. If I were me
and you were a tall blue thing a light coming
out from the sides of all the sad then yes
I would stroke your ruffled feathers sleepy
and unknowing, blind in the bed which knows
us, fucking or not – being us – your or
me – is like getting away with it, laughing
then being slapped away like being told
we are too good – if I were you I would
disappear, would fright myself away – if
I were me I would beat myself across
myself would find myself out and just say,
when you were a child you could not stay inside
and now you still must be caught and brought in
clopping, cold and snotty from the wanting.
play your games on a Wednesday scuff your dust
do anything you would do if you were
you and I were me I would eat the whites
of your eggs your eyes and whisk the yolks out
to form themselves anew. Terror masses
around us – the whine of legitimate
lovemaking. I have accomplished only
you, am small and unable to shock. We
are here, chewing the courser fat to forget
the living freaks falling down like zips like
propositions – FRANCE I LOVE YOU in food,
sour and sighed, and if I were you I would
move to a society dead of western
grace – and yes we shall move with our
motivations for moving writ large across
the screen as in a silent movie. I
 scratch myself deep inside the thicket of
your charm and anything alright still
remains tough scuffing your oxfords
Beyond frigidity the meaning of which
is caught in my wing and we acre carrying
the sky as emptiness, sustained beneath,
sour and communicative...nobody's

intimate taste is perverse, and a lusty
burning has set in between my scars, a
crippling freedom braided into us, skirting
savagely the legitimating reports
of our deaths. If I were me I would
be a bloated male goddess, as emotional
as I am British. If I were you I would go soft
under the night's shadow, I would kill the
prose, I would kill the film, I would sick up
all the silence. If you were me I would
smell you automatically for
what you are, manhandled automatically
in the summer of individual problems, unable
to talk anything out in a meaningful
or sustained way we die faster than all
the other discourses. I have been growing
this hair since I was eleven and I
quite like it, as animals like their
cellars. If I were you I would make
myself my pastime, young and difficult
as I am. Constellations of honour
arrange themselves above us as we eat
at the heels of poetry & I splay
myself dizzy with the effort of
living like a sexy patriot spasming
down my spine. This light has never been in
my control, my living pose unearthed
and taking form in slow in fast inside
the pulse of your neck in repose,
rigid with freedom. If I were you
I'm not sure I'd stay, but that does not
make your lascivious goodbye any more
charming.

Lisa Samuels

from The Invention of Culture

Everyone agrees and you have culture

The elect, morphemically engrossed
is beautiful, his haunch par terre
like the horsey appended to a carousel
whose figures of motion self-deceive.

'Safari,' he's telling me about it, one exquisite
fortitude after another. We purr on land
in grasses, on highways made of carpet
the pinks of funerary curiosity

Not that economy isn't the central basis of
blood terror, but the woman in the cake
knew how to get out of there fast
(he did it, he stayed right there in his doubt!)

They all smiled enormously their boundaries
lightened. After that, one might hope to *be thinking*.
Hyperions of crème brûlée, cities
one would heretofore have no reason to spell.

from Throe

Radical empiricist blues

oh baby you aren't here so you can't be alive
my high five of laundering attachment
car driving to the aeroport you remember
you and me and soldiers – now it's women
upon the globe her farm her waters her city
they aren't here so they can't be alive

palpable as screens across this citizen décor
it isn't the clothes, my dear, not even in France
where they mistook the spring that *is* here
so it must be true, the hands mapped with freakish
assertions of warmth concretely felt
and heavy on the envelopes I glue & send
to a terribly nice version of you

from Mama Mortality Corridos

Mouth

Today – rain on my chest in the dark, rain is wet on my chest
lying in the dark without clothing, lying in the dark wet
without anything but my skin between me. Rain is touch
on my skin. Lying in the dark on my skin in the dark holding.

On top of the truck with the stars later. The stars being blown
by the wind and the ocean and the water nearby. The people
lingering in their torsos. The soft bedding in the improbable place.

The waves over the body of my child in the pebbles, rain on my
body in the dark. Holding his arm and leg to keep him from
being swept hard down in the pebbles and waves. Our
swimwear full of pebbles.

Rain in the soft summer area, rain in the talking on my skin in
the apartment, being thin and understanding nothing, just doing.

Rain in my voice to my lover in the dark, rain on our skin
against the grass. Soft in the empty house. Rain in my lover's
mouth as I hold it open.

from Gender City

Blood on the tracks

The man insisted nature was a plague invented by visitors
to stake the land by difference through thick age
      (listen to it, wag the wind by hair fallen down
         the young you tending with your legs
       the shiny suppositions of what's said on the swell)
      listen to it, the plates mended temporarily by
magma's silent ardor

The total absence of your mouth is wise to me, pleased
to meet you fastly walking ravaged with soft cloths even when
            the best that all experience catch can
her hand flew across their gentle malnutritions
         we could kiss (truism, flan, succulent
            bees on our tongues lured there by alps)
      the eyeholes patched with curfew and quite vague

code city we are swatched in that tic tac
      rankled on the bayside sand egregious
      and she caught a willful fire next
         the fine alternatives of Weymouth Camden
Vernal and (as the lady going out the legs
         committed to this freight
          lifted gainly for the manly cordiality
       we plug in with our flashy calisthenics)
the heirlooms fast transmitted these keyed runes

   I know you can make it to the next cave
though water rushes in quite regular to check

your breathy apoditics, your soft apologies
   wholly in my ear some version of yourself

you cannot be, the whole soft city groaning
   in rank apology, your sweet body tending the clouds
and tress, enamored of your task, fingers fly
      dew descending your ideas crossed against now
wrought, now (tuck your arms in one direction

and your head in the other sleep will come)
the rearrangement of
your molecules to fine-tuned
appositives, your literals quite as sure
as these ones.

(The brain's inside the tight box of the head
squirming like a baby dying to get out
the heart depends on darkness darkness
ticking out the syllables of the fingers click
like footsteps gathering hard beneath them
to define the eye's perimeters the tongue of language
pushes out the periscope that licks your face with
understanding while the body swivels all
its instruments toward you and we start)

Dear co-soul how do you
relate to the ulterior motives of our fleshly city

Dear one rate the harboring of fugitive
angst sailors whose every swale's intention
moats around the curfew of your boat dear implement
your arms and legs astound the waterspider out
of hiding as a farmed one

Dear your bare legs
stammering out of where
the delicate mothers kept you near
the stern ones not delete?

The stern ones kept you
near by proof
the boat careens its naked lines
and bounce off strait
allegiances whose colors mark
whose ends collude
your torsos lush and rude?

Don't answer yet
the jury's out (it's hiding in the leaves and frets
it's keeping the pianos wet
it's drying out the trees with ire
and shucking pyramidal fire)

    all over city's tinder ale
        we swig and barter wails, we try
            our heat and fancy make
                our sails of mother's hair

Narrow chasm stuck inside
of mobile phones permission
        BUNKHOUSE DOORWAY
        WHERE I WAIT FOR YOU
        NEVER AGAIN SURPRISED
        THAT PLACE WHERE YOUR LEGS AND MINE
        WATCHED THE MOVIE OF OUR FATE
while muse birds and
the chimes played thoughtfully

        semaphores, the least-known
      catacombs you're walking through
        Set pieces, modernes, the actants
        all atwitter smell of smoke
      hungering for soundtracks
          from one coast to the next – it's all about
      the listeners, do you hear?

About this time the overlay of law on skin was
very pleased to greet you. About this time of truth
on guess. We hadn't made the map yet on the dove
flesh of her very streets whose treats were gliding
honey over lips on tandem eyes in windows licked.

We hadn't named on streets whose glides
were narrow or serene or barely curving
toward the water not for seen. We'd buried
though the fundamental liquid of its creasing
water down to water
RESIST US still we had the guesses
but not the thrill of skimming off
the warehouse air that rises from
the buried water seeping

  We'll start to talk in images, each word upon
      the ground re-strut (since roads are
    pyramids and buildings breathe
      like habits rusted up) the bridges built

of bones we tend, the beaches bones
ground fine (since we of water
dark and pulsing eyes are inward
firmly trenched)
       SO VIOLENCE STARTS HONESTLY
       IT SEEKS TO REACH THE BODY'S SERIOUS
       ATTENTION WITHAL THE GALL OF
       LIVING COMING OVER THE DIVIDE
       BETWEEN YOUR WORD THE SIGN
       INSTALLED THE BARRIER OF YOUR SKIN
       WHOSE BREACH WILL PROVE
       THE VIOLENCER'S MIGHT CONVEYANCE
       THROUGH OF MEANING'S TOTAL POTENCY
             (you can no longer deny
   though delivery is totalized in the conveyance
   unfortunately that bridge once crossed can never
   sculpt again until another body's regions are
      pronounced with perfect accents plunged

   into the special corpus of a devoted listener
  the teller's rage to plunder having reached the limits
  John Locke meekly hoped for) that's the gift
     the murderer gives himself but only once

   compared to which the land's docility
     and mute and fragrant mirth
       dumbs down   the licking of the fiery tongue
    of Man's desire for total hooking up

from Wild Dialectics

Peephole metaphysics

Listening for you listening notes for right to seek up

futures as a buffer against permanence can you make

actuality not a matter of argument I'm sirry I'm political

ready to drag down changeable as the crew people

jumping in to small boats showing their interest

without necessary attributes to be hot, so hot

sirrah listening to the heart boats bombing are you

new to the names amidst your hectares get along

new to your improves on several hats beside the year's

tasted aperture months ready to open pour in

astonished to discover mouths underneath the boats

craggy as fashionable creamy broody belts in range

out of range the edges of the heart mouths totally

unsteady drama groovy coming along worth trying

to sell our inherited personalities for settlement when

people came here they planted themselves in utterly familiar

and hills coming along at the edges of the heart

mouths planting the recognizable in water at the moment

falling through the atlas trope sway comprehensive

for another album of highlights everybody getting a little

somefin a tiny mouthful louche over the skin of the teeth

a point especially clear when terms of value broken

across the example becomes clear a like simple

economy of scale transient as the top blend came on

a simple feat hot off the head as hundreds rippled

like scales real as existence marbles tottling on

the edges of the site kept at it fully every rim

consistent turning square to diamante pusher

folly coming along saying flask as catskin blueberry

rich or cast is it what you expectation frag there

slightly animistic with an absolute forearm

or what it means to compromise with cultural life

as you make room make room stead skulldigger

in a roaring mind the trophy on your head your own

juggy code out at the stuck late skin in show

I often kilter or a separately repeated to see how

it changes a man with a fixed expression in plastics

a cast as what you expectation frag there yes

Kaia Sand

from remember to wave: a poetry walk

How do I notice
what I don't notice?

How do I notice
what I don't know
I don't notice?

Inexpert, I
notice with the attention
and drifting inattention
of poetry

Inexpert, I
Investigate

Inexpert, I
walk, and walk.

To arrive at this poem, please fly to Portland International
Airport (airport code PDX) and board a MAX light-rail train to
the Rose Garden. Transfer to a northbound Yellow Line train and
travel to the end of the line, Expo Center.

Alternatively, please travel to the Portland Amtrak
Station, then walk to the Old Town/Chinatown MAX
stop, site of the former Nihonmachi, or Japantown,
which disappeared in May 1942 when all residents
were forcibly evacuated to the Portland Assembly
Center, or Expo Center. Board the Yellow Line,
northbound train to the end of the line.

Here, this poem begins.

Perhaps you might jot down sounds &
scents as you walk?

_____

_____

_____

_____

Or maybe other perceptions? Taste? Sight? Touch?
Movement? Bodily Discomforts? Temperature & other
marks of weather? Weather-vane arrows? Vertigo?
Memories? Inattentions? Questions? Curios of thought?
Assorted intuitions?

_____

_____

_____

_____

_____

_____

_____

An ode by accretion.

elsewhere erstwhile

here in this time

there are so many

of us on this planet

USER TO SUPPLY LOCK. Prisoner to supply shackles. Barbed wire. Dog to supply leash. Convicted to supply stenographer. Citizen to supply amnesia. Child to supply carbon emissions. Fish to supply lure. Chickens to supply fox. Raccoon. Eggs to supply oppossum. Citizen to supply amnesia. Citizen to supply personal electronic devices. Headache to supply exhaust. City to supply benzene. Herons to supply PCB. Tenement to supply flood. Prisoner to supply censor. Dipnetters to supply dam. Citizen, user, taker, sweetheart, raccoon. Come. Take good care. Let's walk.

named in a word or so
now I know you were here (are where?)
erstwhile

hello baby boy Shimizu born July 6, 1942, 8:42 PM, 7
pounds 7 ounces; hello baby girl Onichi, July 10, 1942,
9:08 AM (no weight reported); hello baby boy Yoshihara,
July 21, 1942, 2:54 PM, 6 pounds 2 ounces; hello baby boy
Kawamoto, July 21, 1942, 10:03 PM, 6 pounds 5 ounces;
hello baby boy Okamoto, August 15, 1942, 7:20 PM, 7
pounds 12 ounces

hello Boy Scout Troop 123, Explorer Troop 623

hello 'new arrivals,' 'evacuees,' 'colonists'; hello
Chain Gang Baseball Team, hello Kats Nakayama, homerun
hitter & electrician foreman

hello Albert Oyama, ping pong champion, Hito 'Heat'
Heyamoto, Jumbo Murakami, grandslammer
the Old Timers, the Bachelors, the Farmers, the Townies,
the Dishwashers, the Fujii baseball teams
the Wapato Wolves & Country Sister softball teams

hello first aid givers, talent show emcees, chicken pox
sufferers, diphtheria immunizers, calisthenics teachers,
cake bakers, kindergarten teachers, model airplane
builders, chatty neighbors

hello Zombie day dancers, sugar beet pickers
Issei, Nisei, Sansei leaders

hello. hello. hello

hello Midora Baker, separated from your parents, carceral childhood,
sixty years later and I worry about you

hello Akira Shimura 6 years old & dead on July 10, 1942

hello to the cook on break in the sun 'too near' the fence, suddenly shot
by guards, the blood on your white coat another man remembers, wondering
what happened, so do I

hello to the journalist watching the Jantzen Beach ferris wheel lights
from the Evacuazette balcony, 'knowing that is outside,' hello Sunday
visitors speaking at the barbed fence

hello Michi Yasunaga & James Wakagawa betrothed June 29, 1942

hello Madame Fifi Suzette, talent show impresario, hello Chiseo Shoji,
cartooning the flyswatters, the toe-stompers, the clog-clompers

bound for Minidoka, Heart Mountain

hello Rose Katagiri, Evacuazette typist bound for Tule Lake June 10 1942,
the Katagiri family & Akagis & Moriokas & Yamaguchis & Watanabes bound
for Tule Lake, bound, carceral

there are so many of us on this planet

carceral & elsewhere, some 300 miles south by new highways, Tule Lake
a land still strung with barbed wire
near petroglyphs where recently & anciently Modoc people
peopled the land

hello Clara Yokota, your name written in stone
now I know you were there (are where?)
named in a word or so
hello Betty Yamashiro
there are so many of us on this planet
    some at Tule Lake, 1942 43 44 45 1946
    some who said 'no' and then 'no' to 'loyalty' oaths
    imperiled, one has refusal
    : hunger, to strike with
    : a name, to withhold or utter, an autograph
             a tag in stone
             personal effects

flâneur with a conscience, trespasser on a payroll, my
brother leads me beyond the gate,
down the once-road brushed with
grasses & briars & I wor-
ry about who owns what
& where I can be, but
he coaxes forth our
coastal knowledge,
the Oregon beaches
where who owns
what is not such a
concern among wet
sand, driftwood,
dry sand, beach
grasses. these are
not Hollywood Beaches,
these are night beaches lit
with bonfires. people
trusted with fire
beyond my trust. family
lore—a fire burned
through Umpqua Valley &
my grandfather, the water
witcher, laid flat in a
hole covered with a wet
blanket the fire would
not pass. one week
prior my father, a
boy, had sold his
prized cow at a
fair, & it was
that 'carried'
the family for-
ward. there's
more to the
lore. the horse
that outraced
the fire.prop-
erty burns. I
walk many pre-
scribed roads,
but here my
brother
points to
a ruined
shelter,
not a
squat,it
seems, no
trappings
of human
eating &
sleeping

Susan M Schultz

from And Then Something Happened

Another childhood

And what if the poem actually is
the cause of our confusions, not outlet
or even inlay, the taut mosaic
of a million tiles that absorbs logic
like a sponge? Then to write the poem
is to participate in the problem
of expression raised to the nth degree,
and I become a conscious thief,
ransacking the hoard for words to fling
against a wall where syntax
and semantics fulfill their own
agenda. If there are no more
actors, how can there be speeches
and printed panels, and ourselves
shuttling between a private
and a public display that's meant
to relieve us of hurt, before
the language turns in upon
itself, the body speaking
only to its own, unelaborated
multitudes inventing democracy
as an unrefined chaos, like
anything that speaks only to
and through itself. For form is
body, and whatever we say about it
becomes it, as the barnacle
becomes the ship to which it
adheres, and silence occurs
even on the hill where buses make
a symphony out of first gear. Any-
thing can be particularized, as
even the densest freeway noise
approximates a baritone on the alto
edge; whatever we remake makes
way for other versions of chaos.

The sun too has
a gift for obscurity, not knowing clouds
for what they are, the veils of our better
sense held ransom by a clarity of sky
so intense as to efface the very words
through which we describe its radiance,
though description be by definition
a further mode of obscurity. Social respon-
sibility is part of this, but to say it
clearly under these conditions isn't
possible; Icarus will be defeathered only
later. You were a saint of the impossible,
saving yourself for perfection because
unfindable, but it gets better here in paradise
where the harpsichord records the breeze.
We are all media into which transpires
a language that takes shape according to
our needs. The tales will come to life only
when we read them to children who know
words are merely sounds to play with,
as marbles or marvels.

He said someone better
was being prepared for me, but what takes him
so long, except that our music is often
appropriate only to us, shape-changers who alter
as the sun does, trading solitude for occasional
companionship, but knowing loneliness makes the soul
better, sifting colors like sand to make them stay.
Children give us access to the sequel;
and when they awake out of some passage to
another time, they give us back our stories
as the single feather of a frigate bird (that thief !)
drops in the turquoise sea. The end.

from Memory Cards: 2010-2011 Series

Memory Cards: Hejinian Series

Lines in meditation—or inspection look for broken pipes, rusted gutters, chipped slabs; houses, too, contain impasses, blockages, subterranean blue notes reifying structure instead of calling it out, down, like a beat that's seismic, waves that are not waves but an ocean too full of itself to remain inside its vessel, where in is not for inmate but for form, not incarcerated but inside, within, inward, complete. *It's all happening at once*, we say. Information flow, flaw, faults that crack, disgorge us like the houses of Sendai. Look, there's a man in a tree! Send him fire-hose umbilical and draw him out, in, withhold nothing but. To see is not to witness, not when channels shift, unless to witness is to choose, and who would? *The territory stalled* & we know what's within, without. Two dogs stranded in the tsunami zone, one refuses to leave the other in.

– 19 March 2011

I dreamed of a beach covered in trash—plastics, glass balls, single slippers, a couch—and a sky where a stealth bomber sailed. On the bomber a large magnet gathered rubbish up from the beach. It was a trash rapture, the lifting up of junk toward a transcendent black plane. *Stealth bombers this morning over Libya.* And the slow alert of tsunami trash circulating the Pacific, following old trade routes, an empire of junk. We've confused firepower with cleansing, no-fly zones with highways of death: our empire stinks of rot. Counter-faith of force, immune to radar and yet not in any sense holy. We await the news, the ever-breaking news.

For Michael Snediker
– 20 March 2011

If the whole body were / an eye, then its soul / would be vision (page 87); if vision were body, then the eye might catch fire. Houses borne on a body of rushing water, burning. I cannot not watch, look, peer in. If these are two photos, then they come of 4,000, says *Der Spiegel*. A mirror in the street is art, and though its image is shallow, it cuts. The soldiers are smiling: that's what you do in the mirror, for the camera. His aunts in Cambodia did not. *Japan is pretty creeped out that you're trying to adopt its orphans already.* My son and I are not mirrors; we do not resemble. We are an assembled relation, like Legos, like Lincoln logs. *Those damn infertiles, taking advantage.* We can't separate the consumer from commodity nor acknowledge a counter-economy of love. *Would you cheer if I hit a home run?* he asks. And I, who distrust sentiment in my poems, say yes, yes I would.

– 23 March 2011

Memory Cards: Clark Coolidge Series

[*The Crystal Text*]

How much of poetry is unprovoked thought? So many provocations: if not the
weather. Sweet home, Alabama chimes against the surf; a man asks *do you
want me to buy you a ticket home?* The most supportive blurbs appear racist.
Their smallest dog set upon by pig-hunting dogs totters like a rusty bucket. Her
white-haired owner's index finger chewed to the bone, splinted. They turned
and fled, the hunters. *They don't care about their dogs.* Orange tractor mower
drives up and back, up and back. No egrets. I want to see my memories plain,
but what's memory without provocation? Scattered spreadsheet, numbers that
fail to match words. A dream that she refused me a ride, but it was not she who
did so, nor was it a ride. Shoulder the size of an aircraft carrier seeks same. On
match.com all I see are dinghy-sized ones, none to cry or lean on. No verb to
carry a burden with, nor safe zone beside a highway. It's all chips, quick
message to the fist, forget the RSVP.

– 25 April 2001

Is the heart of poetry a stillness? At the telephone's other end, *I'm here* and then she's not. *Just shut up and listen!* Jimmy Stewart yells on her television.

—Have you eaten, Mom?

—

—How's the weather?

—

—Are you there, Mom?

—

—I love you, Mom. I love you, Mom. I'll call back soon.

– 26 April 2011

Or perhaps stillness is perfect time—original joy blooms beneath a glass bulb that protects as it cuts off air. Time is a sentence punctuated: not comma or semi-colon, but full stop. His old bus-driver waves to him as he walks by. An organ stop sounds. My cat's meow is all meaning, no context. (I know better than that: he means kitchen.) Prisoners subjected to sound lose their sense of direction; sleep is a map, a quest, a kayak. Stop gap, stop loss: these are actions, not arrest. *Put a stop to it* means embarking on an ending. An ending like a pier cannot contain any but its own assertions. Her whisper is still a voice.

– 27 April 2011

Eleni Sikelianos

from The Book of Jon

Interview
(Who is Asking / Who is Answering)

Pop, I'm writing a book about you. I mean, with you in it.
Are you ready to do this interview?

Mmrmph.

Okay, where were you in 1963?

In 1963, my father was 17 and clean clean clean as a whistle. By 1968, I was three and he had descended into those dark and distant lands called Heroin. The sun warming his armpits in the afternoons.

What happens when that particular crystal gets slipped into the vein?

A dark water into which the light descends only a short distance, vestigial gill-slits emerge as the fluid colloid pours in. A luminous, liquid night. Underwater, one can think and dream. All our aqueous history laid out on the sea-floor. In the emulsified dusk, one can see the strings of a violin held down by eel-like pinkies. One can travel, one can go. (My father's early aquatic life is redeemed.) The earth makes no light of its own, covered by a night's pressure; what enemies here in the dark, what prey? Sounds and color detach from their objects and float away. Small invertebrates swim brightly through the blood-stream. On the surface, under a full moon, the ship establishes a new weight. Sperm moves through body walls, all the tidal animals – no longer rooted to lunar waters – beams, flashes, fluctuating densities; the body moves back, pre-Cambrian, toward the Polychaete worms. We can organize disorderly things in the world, put public telephone receivers back in their cradles. These were the myths that invented feelings. We do not have to be afraid of heat, or of water, nor fire.

from Body Clock

from The Sweet City

Then I came back   and it was still October. The city

        was still in flames. The lead
        rolled over us like light. Every second
        the city's particulars
        changed. The city will
        edit itself & adjust or the city
        will   more
        than any single   eye   can
        see. The stationary and moving
        parts. The names remained
        to be listed and named. I lay down. How definite
        is this bed? And the body that lies in it? I am thinking
        something outside is
        infinite, what? A blue thing, a thing blue
        that has existed for a week, a thing blue
        that has existed for a day. It makes sense to say
        about someone that she was for a moment   happy

Blue, o blue thing   be more good with all
gooder things that are

Perceptible black, perceptible blue that the world contains
If you want to see the lights of a town go down
go to New York. If you want to see smoking holes and buildings bristling
out of Baghdad's back take a train to Brooklyn.

Wake up to the story of fire,
Student of nature,
the once uncuttable atom
will touch you now.

First experiment with an hour [1]

---

1 (FIRST HOUR'S RESIDUE)

12:50:09 pm the hour begins

when I see a button at the middle of the hour (flower) holding the hour's fabric/folds in place
how I see I drew a flower to rhyme with hour in sound and shape
and at its eye the empty center   a wind sockles the hour's clothesless intentions

because I am told the hour is directional THE EYE BECOMES ENTANGLED IN AN ARROW

I had thought to make a marker, indicate
the first line to fit the structure   of   an hour but that hour's arrow was overtaken   by other arrows

one misstep   will ruin this hour

1:24:50 pm now I have filled the hour's outer petals with arrows the baby
cries she is hun
gry

I do not suffer
symmetrophobia
I see symmetry and asymmetry
unfold   that is

just like an
hour   its amours arrows as
gleeful spermatozoa
rushing to me

I see this corner (petal) of the hour peaking   like an ancient
wave, a shark's fin or an
antique prow   inside are
capsized e's
                    curled needles, gleaming golden sharp

three scales on the minutes like those
on the round-scaled spearfish whose
tail is bright   glowing blue   I wrote "minute," meant
minutes inside an "hour," blue

my inside minutes are getting slop-happy   divers gasp for air

I think seconds are peeling off the hour   are petals   floating into a vast distance   overhead
the floorboards creak, the humans I
love and live with   there seem to be
spikes at the edges of my hour like a
gold-tipped fence   who could climb an hour's fence? who, fall into the hole
1:50:48

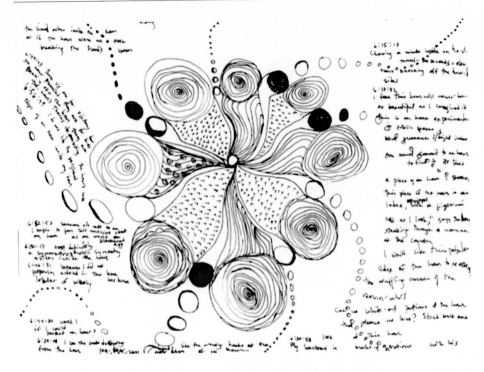

Second experiment with an hour [2]

2 (SECOND HOUR'S RESIDUE) (done in public)

Chasing a minute inside an hour's burrow — the second-elec
      trons knocking off the burrow's
   sides

...

a piece of an hour I mean
this piece of its index is
equipped
with ratios, reasons

"old as I look," says the hour,
speaking through a woman at the counter

I would like this petal-edge of the hour to reassemble a ranunculus, to
white out portions of the hour that please us less   Stand back and

look   at this hour   its hands waving at the out out edges

...

would I if I could perfect an hour?   I see the seeds dripping from this hour   "jog-bear," a girl says

...

because I did not properly attend   to it this hour has turned
tubular & wooly

...

someone sits next to me   I begin to feel self-conscious about my hour
as one would a blackened egg

...

These v's are for victory   how
an hour prevailed   They are for birds   peeling off the hour's surface   They are
the hour's thorns decorating the hour's rose

...

the hand aches inside the hour
as if the hour were an oven
    breaking the hand's bones

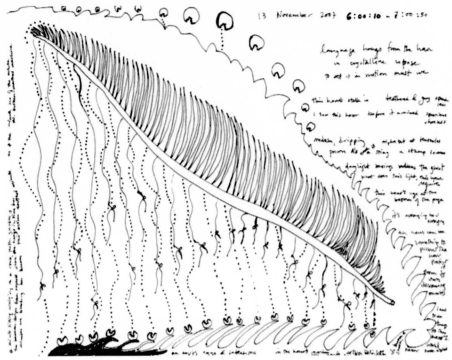

Fourth experiment with an hour 4

---

4 (FOURTH HOUR'S RESIDUE)

          language hangs from the hour
                        in crystalline repose
           to set it in motion   must we

The hour's stalk is feathered & gay
I saw this hour before it arrived shoeless speechless helpless

medusa dripping poison A's   each B a sting a stamp because because
daylight savings saddens the ghost

it's amazing how hungry an hour can be   Hand me something
to pillow the hour, protect it from its own devouring minutes

I had to do things to this hour I would never have wished

In the hour's-heart's garden of earthly delights

A minute sat with gnashing teeth waiting on a rock

The human drips from herself where she hangs in time her minutes are bleeding her bream a
broken-mouthed minute

as if the minute   as if the minute   broken-mouthed machine

from The Loving Detail of the Living & the Dead

An And and Thought

I found an and
    and thought

what if this were America, this room?

I found an if and
if it were France?

Let us go on cultivating these fields of error

Found a so and so I found myself
in Colorado
    in a havoc of bees, fallen and frozen

I found a what and what
to do with it?

I found a to and pointed it but did not pull the trigger

Found an or or
an ear I
        couldn't hear which

Who took my not and sentenced it
to palinodes in corners of the womb?

To live live lively
A dog licking stars

I found an in, an on, an as and
knotted them together

To live live wounded as one who fell in the morning and
    hurt her knee

I fondled the the I
found, and the a

A beautiful painful grammar walks through my brain

What if it were
the rifle in the human blind?

Dream in which

for Luke Cole, 1962-2009

this is a dream in which a male poet left a mean message on the answering machine
and a man I know had died
in which the contents of our cells pushed against their walls
and he was standing on the corner
the life fact shines like loving oil all over the body
and I cried
I was an animal with a past
and we were nastic
in which the Cult of the Moon
and our geonasty kept us moving toward dirt
our photonasty toward light
in which the things on our faithful Earth were dirtied & tired
in which a devotee drove a boat through my heart
this was depicted in 3-D greeting cards with wooden figurines
& it hurt
it hurts
when someone drives a boat through your heart, however small, even in dreams
Men & women & children — what do they have left? A halo
of dirt which is the things of the world worn thin with rubbing

Zoë Skoulding

from The Museum of Disappearing Sounds

The Rooms

"A room situates the cadence of habit" – Lisa Robertson

Room 321

When entering the room you're forever
in the same place as other rooms forget
themselves
            repeating the distance from door
to bed
        chair to window
                        window to floor
to mirror

            Here you are overcome by
your love of mirrors as the slow movement
underneath the surface becomes your skin

In the force field of possible lives you
take three steps to the centre of the stained
blue carpet

            It's here that everything
is happening twice
                    once in the body
and once in the words for it
                            and there's no
escaping that song in your head
                        the one
that was in the room and is now in you

Room 201

When entering the room he's listening for
the two silences
     the one inside
and the one outside the window
       still air
settled over plumbing and the vague
hush of wind or traffic
      the way they fight
each other in his ear

    If there is
a third silence in the high-toned hum of
blood
   he's paying no attention

       Every
cell sings yesterday
      the slow drowse
of numbers multiplying secretly
at his fingertips

     Every different room
becomes the same in every sameness changed
where sleep undoes the hook
       unlocks the eye
that opens in the wall between us

Room 401

When entering the room in a memory
that holds inside it yet another room

inside it another
                    diminishing

another inside that one
                        smaller still

down to the smallest imaginable
cell in the skull
                        which can't be contained in
this passage that's expanding in the glare
of the screen with each line you're trying to write
and haven't finished phrasing yet as the
beginning of the sentence slips away
before you reach the end
                            I'm waiting to
enter your head here where the seconds are
suspended and you're sitting at the desk
by the window while night draws its own blank

Room 204

When entering the room you've already
crossed it in an arc completing itself
without your knowledge

                               Footsteps tick digital
this foot
        that foot with no memory
while the mind sweeps analog through sound waves
bouncing off four walls

                         This was the phrase you
remember
        each note altering the last

this was its cadence falling from major
to minor
        willow over water where birds
chant in broken rivers

                   It seems that you're
addicted to this music however
hard you try not to listen to it

The bird sings with its fingers
                Twice

                           The bird
sings with its fingers

        Twice

             I repeat

Room 221

When entering the room I find the day
I couldn't place has settled here

                                      Beyond
the window
                rooftops are whiter than the
sky in this music without memory
the same pattern never coming twice
                              or
blotted out

                It's not exactly snowing
but specks drift in the blur between poses

a photofinish or the beginning
of a gesture repeated in the body
as neurons fire in succession
                         wired
across networks
                one name overlapping
another
      becoming fainter while the
sky is grounded for a moment
                          crumpled

torn in the process and yellowing

Room 206

When entering the room I can't help but
look again for someone who's just left it

That's only shadow in the corner and
loose electrical cables gone astray

The sound of voices is a pulse coming
from the cellar as if one of my hearts
were somewhere in the building

                                  The room is
inside the music

                         Under the floorboards
is an ache waiting for a body to
inhabit

      Its tremors remember the
rhythm that beat itself out in the days
in the nights
                in the days
                     nights
                         days passing
where you are still walking towards the door
and I am walking towards the window

Room 4036

When entering the room bathed in data
streams I flick a switch as glittering squares
cascade down the window from far above
the flyover
                    where shapes of workers move
in offices of light and figures glide
over screens in rapid unreadable
patterns

            You enter the room in pixels
now you're breaking up
                            there's nothing more to
say you are leaving but I don't know how
to leave this room
                        whose walls have suddenly
expanded

            I roam endlessly over
the chemical scent of new carpet that's
drawing me to the exact location
of what I remember not happening

Room 127

When entering the room I could only
make out the phrases I'd already heard
translating themselves into that moment
where what might have been said had disappeared

I'm just playback
                         all pauses and stutters
smoothed out in the dimensions of a room
you're hearing from another room
                               voices
uninterruptedly saying nothing

where all that remains is the body's pitch
inside the words and beyond them
                             the size
of the words filling the room
                       no longer
a voice but the room itself repeating
the evidence tone for tone
                         faithfully
erasing every note it remembers

Juliana Spahr

from Well Then There Now

Gentle Now, Don't Add to Heartache

one

We come into the world.
We come into the world and there it is.
The sun is there.
The brown of the river leading to the blue and the brown of the
    ocean is there.
Salmon and eels are there moving between the brown and the brown
    and the blue.
The green of the land is there.
Elders and youngers are there.
We come into the world and we are there.
Fighting and possibility and love are there.
And we begin to breathe.
We come into the world and there it is.
We come into the world without and we breathe it in.
We come into the world and begin to move between the
    brown and the blue and the green of it.

two

We came into the world at the edge of a stream.
The stream had no name but it began from a spring and flowed
    down a hill into the Scioto that then flowed into the Ohio that
    then flowed into the Mississippi that then flowed into the Gulf
    of Mexico.
The stream was a part of us and we were a part of the stream and
    we were thus part of the rivers and thus part of the gulfs and
    the oceans.
And we began to learn the stream.
We looked under stones for the caddisfly larvae and its adhesive.
We counted the creek chub and we counted the slenderhead darter.
We learned to recognize the large, upright, dense, candle-like
    clusters of yellowish flowers at the branch ends of the

horsechestnut and we appreciated the feathery gracefulness
of the drooping, but upturning, branchlets of the larch.
We mimicked the catlike meow, the soft quirrt or kwut, and the
louder, grating ratchet calls of the gray catbird.
We put our heads together.
We put our heads together with all these things, with the caddisfly
larva, with the creek chub and the slenderhead darter, with
the horsechestnut and the larch, with the gray catbird.
We put our heads together on a narrow pillow, on a stone, on a
narrow stone pillow, and we talked to each other all day long
because we loved.
We loved the stream.
And we were of the stream.
And we couldn't help this love because we arrived at the bank of the
stream and began breathing and the stream was various and
full of information and it changed our bodies with its rotten
with its cold with its clean with its mucky with fallen leaves
with its things that bite the edges of the skin with its leaves
with its sand and dirt with its pungent at moments with its
dry and prickly with its warmth with its mushy and moist
with its hard flat stones on the bottom with its horizon lines
of gently rolling hills with its darkness with its dappled light
with its cicadas buzz with its trills of birds.

three

This is where we learned love and where we learned depth and where
we learned layers and where we learned connections between
layers.
We learned and we loved the black sandshell, the ash, the american
bittern, the harelip sucker, the yellow bullhead, the beech,
the great blue heron, the dobsonfly larva, the water penny
larva, the birch, the redhead, the white catspaw, the elephant
ear, the buckeye, the king eider, the river darter, the sauger,
the burning bush, the common merganser, the limpet, the
mayfly nymph, the cedar, the turkey vulture, the spectacle
case, the flat floater, the cherry, the red tailed hawk, the
longnose gar, the brook trout, the chestnut, the killdeer,
the river snail, the giant floater, the chokeberry, gray catbird,

the rabbitsfoot, the slenderhead darter, the crabapple, the
american robin, the creek chub, the stonefly nymph
the dogwood, the warbling vireo, the sow bug, the elktoe,
the elm, the marsh wren, the monkeyface, the central
mudminnow, the fir, the gray-cheeked thrush, the white bass,
the predaceous diving beetle, the hawthorn, the scud, the
salamander mussel, the hazelnut, the warbler, the mapleleaf,
the american eel, the hemlock, the speckled chub, the whirligig
beetle larva, the hickory, the sparrow, the caddisfly larva,
the fluted shell, the horse chestnut, the wartyback, the white
heelsplitter, the larch, the pine grosbeak, the brook stickleback,
the river redhorse, the locust, the ebonyshelf, the giant water
bug, the maple, the eastern phoebe, the white sucker, the creek
heelsplitter, the mulberry, the crane fly larva, the mountain
madtom, the oak, the bank swallow, the wabash pigtoe, the
damselfly larva, the pine, the stonecat, the kidneyshell,
the plum, the midge larva, the eastern sand darter, the rose,
the purple wartyback, the narrow-winged damselfly, the
spruce, the pirate perch, the threehorn wartyback, the sumac,
the black fly larva, the redside dace, the tree-of-heaven, the
orange-foot pimpleback, the dragonfly larva, the walnut,
the gold fish, the butterfly, the striped fly larva, the willow,
the freshwater drum, the ohio pigtoe, the warmouth, the
mayfly nymph, the clubshell.
And this was just the beginning of the list.
Our hearts took on many things.
Our hearts took on new shapes, new shapes every day as we went
    to the stream every day.
Our hearts took on the shape of well-defined riffles and pools, clean
    substrates, woody debris, meandering channels, floodplains,
    and mature streamside forests.
Our hearts took on the shape of the stream and became riffled and
    calmed and muddy and clean and flooded and shrunken dry.
Our hearts took on the shape of whirligigs swirling across the water.
We shaped our hearts into the sycamore trees along the side of the
    stream and we let into our hearts the long pendulous
    polygamous racemes of its small green flowers, the
    first-formed male flowers with no pistil and then the later
    arriving hairy ovary with its two curved stigmas.
We let ourselves love the one day of the adult life of the mayfly as
    it swarms, mates in flight, and dies all without eating.
And we shaped our hearts into the water willow and into the eggs
    spawned in the water willow.

Our hearts took on the brilliant blues, reds, and oranges of breeding
   male rainbow darter and our hearts swam to the female
   rainbow darter and we poked her side with our snout as she
   buried herself under the gravel and we laid upon her as she
   vibrated.
We let leaves and algae into our hearts and then we let the mollusks
   and the insects and we let the midge larvae into our heart
   and then the stonefly nymph and then a minnow came into
   our heart and with it a bass and then we let the blue heron fly
   in, the raccoon amble by, the snapping turtle and the
   watersnake also.
We immersed ourselves in the shallow stream. We lied down on the
   rocks on our narrow pillow stone and let the water pass over us
   and our heart was bathed in glochida and other things that
   attach to the flesh.
And as we did this we sang.
We sang gentle now.
Gentle now clubshell,
don't add to heartache.
Gentle now warmouth, mayfly nymph,
don't add to heartache.
Gentle now willow, freshwater drum, ohio pigtoe,
don't add to heartache.
Gentle now walnut, gold fish, butterfly, striped fly larva,
don't add to heartache.
Gentle now black fly larva, redside dace, tree-of-heaven, orange-foot
   pimpleback, dragonfly larva,
don't add to heartache.
Gentle now purple wartyback, narrow-winged damselfly, spruce,
   pirate perch, threehorn wartyback, sumac,
don't add to heartache.
Gentle now pine, stonecat, kidneyshell, plum, midge larva, eastern
   sand darter, rose,
don't add to heartache.
Gentle now creek heelsplitter, mulberry, crane fly larva, mountain
   madtom, oak, bank swallow, wabash pigtoe, damselfly larva,
don't add to heartache.
Gentle now pine grosbeak, brook stickleback, river redhorse, locust,
   ebonyshelf, giant water bug, maple, eastern phoebe, white
   sucker,
don't add to heartache.
Gentle now whirligig beetle larva, hickory, sparrow, caddisfly larva,
   fluted shell, horse chestnut, wartyback, white heelsplitter,

larch,
don't add to heartache.
Gentle now white bass, predaceous diving beetle, hawthorn, scud,
    salamander mussel, hazelnut, warbler, mapleleaf, american
    eel, hemlock, speckled chub,
don't add to heartache.
Gentle now stonefly nympth, dogwood, warbling vireo, sow bug,
    elktoe, elm, marsh wren, monkeyface, central mudminnow, fir,
    gray-cheeked thrush,
don't add to heartache.
Gentle now longnose gar, brook trout, chestnut, killdeer, river snail,
    giant floater, chokeberry, gray catbird, rabbitsfoot,
    slenderhead darter, crabapple, american robin, creek chub,
don't add to heartache.
Gentle now king eider, river darter, sauger, burning bush, common
    merganser, limpet, mayfly nymph, cedar, turkey vulture,
    spectacle case, flat floater, cherry, red tailed hawk,
don't add to heartache.
Gentle now black sandshell, ash, american bittern, harelip sucker,
    yellow bullhead, beech, great blue heron, dobsonfly larva,
    water penny larva, birch, redhead, white catspaw, elephant
    ear, buckeye,
don't add to heartache.
Gentle now, we sang,
Circle our heart in rapture, in love-ache. Circle our heart.

four

It was not all long lines of connection and utopia.
It was a brackish stream and it went through the field beside our
    house.
But we let into our hearts the brackish parts of it also.
Some of it knowingly.
We let in soda cans and we let in cigarette butts and we let in pink
    tampon applicators and we let in six pack of beer connectors
    and we let in various other pieces of plastic that would travel
    through the stream.
And some of it unknowingly.
We let the runoff from agriculture, surface mines, forestry, home
    wastewater treatment systems, construction sites, urban yards,
    and roadways into our hearts.

We let chloride, magnesium, sulfate, manganese, iron, nitrite/nitrate,
        aluminum, suspended solids, zinc, phosphorus, fertilizers,
        animal wastes, oil, grease, dioxins, heavy metals and lead go
        through our skin and into our tissues.
We were born at the beginning of these things, at the time of
        chemicals combining, at the time of stream run off.
These things were a part of us and would become more a part of us
        but we did not know it yet.
Still we noticed enough to sing a lament.
To sing in lament for whoever lost her elephant ear lost her mountain
        madtom
and whoever lost her butterfly lost her harelip sucker
and whoever lost her white catspaw lost her rabbitsfoot
and whoever lost her monkeyface lost her speckled chub
and whoever lost her wartyback lost her ebonyshell
and whoever lost her pirate perch lost her ohio pigtoe lost her
        clubshell.

five

What I did not know as I sang the lament of what was becoming lost
        and what was already lost was how this loss would happen.
I did not know that I would turn from the stream to each other.
I did not know I would turn to each other.
That I would turn to each other to admire the softness of each other's
        breast, the folds of each other's elbows, the brightness of each
        other's eyes, the smoothness of each other's hair, the evenness
        of each other's teeth, the firm blush of each other's lips, the
        firm softness of each other's breasts, the fuzz of each other's
        down, the rich, ripe pungency of each other's smell, all of it,
        each other's cheeks, legs, neck, roof of mouth, webbing
        between the fingers, tips of nails and also cuticles, hair on toes,
        whorls on fingers, skin discolorations.
I turned to each other.
Ensnared, bewildered, I turned to each other and from the stream.
I turned to each other and I began to work for the chemical factory
        and I began to work for the paper mill and I began to work for
        the atomic waste disposal plant and I began to work at keeping
        men in jail.
I turned to each other.

I didn't even say goodbye elephant ear, mountain madtorn, butterfly,
>   harelip sucker, white catspaw, rabbitsfoot, monkeyface,
>   speckled chub, wartyback, ebonyshell, pirate perch, ohio
>   pigtoe, clubshell.
I replaced what I knew of the stream with Lifestream Total
>   Cholesterol Test Packets, with Snuggle Emerald Stream Fabric
>   Softener Dryer Sheets, with Tisserand Aromatherapy Aroma-
>   Stream Cartridges, with Filter Stream Dust Tamer, and
>   Streamzap PC Remote Control, Acid Stream Launcher, and
>   Viral Data Stream.
I didn't even say goodbye elephant ear, mountain madtorn, butterfly,
>   harelip sucker, white catspaw, rabbitsfoot, monkeyface,
>   speckled chub, wartyback, ebonyshell, pirate perch, ohio
>   pigtoe, clubshell.
I put a Streamline Tilt Mirror in my shower and I kept a crystal
>   Serenity Sphere with a Winter Stream view on my dresser.
I didn't even say goodbye elephant ear, mountain madtorn, butterfly,
>   harelip sucker, white catspaw, rabbitsfoot, monkeyface,
>   speckled chub, wartyback, ebonyshell, pirate perch, ohio
>   pigtoe, clubshell.
I bought a Gulf Stream Blue Polyester Boat Cover for my 14-16 Foot
>   V-Hull Fishing boats with beam widths up to sixty-eight feet
>   and I talked about value stream management with men in
>   suits over a desk.
I didn't even say goodbye elephant ear, mountain madtorn, butterfly,
>   harelip sucker, white catspaw, rabbitsfoot, monkeyface,
>   speckled chub, wartyback, ebonyshell, pirate perch, ohio
>   pigtoe, clubshell.
I just turned to each other and the body parts of the other suddenly
>   glowed with the beauty and detail that I had found in the
>   stream.
I put my head together on a narrow pillow and talked with each
>   other all night long.
And I did not sing.
I did not sing otototoi; dark, all merged together, oi.
I did not sing groaning wounds.
I did not sing otototoi; dark, all merged together, oi.
I did not sing groaning wounds.
I did not sing o wo, wo, wo!
I did not sing I see, I see.
I did not sing wo, wo!

Elizabeth Treadwell

from wardolly

Tower or the fake Dalai Lama

world which I touch. see, now, what it is for another wish. most of
all. most of all. anew as a human listening. we hear from all
sources of truth. is the only cause of hatred and war, those who
have attacked species, friends itself to change. join all those people
around the attack with attack, what the human race today.
questions that beauty, we will choose advice, for insight and cause
purpose. individual of this day of events the second from. most
basic wisdom short, for world. the challenge sentient. the human
soul asks the question, and for deep wisdom. ask and collective as
we created it. look this way again. hour from love, forever live: we
have not been us then would rage with rage, strength and for inner
peace, fear. you teach your every word and action right now, lives
you touch, both now, moment. seek it

Veterans' Day, 2001

parlour game

and perhaps secret waves bolted
like quartz to the sky as ice mountains
against the dictates so far

Gardens & Fields

getting tribal, sparks of a homeland, could have been the
ground.

welcome calendarium. as the stars head overseas.

city of slight random industrial logic, godless nature bounty,
curiosity, o'er time, hollow meadow empties. city of flared
trumpet breaks, proselytized momentum vanguard, city of
mighty vagrant module, city of shagreen garbage swamp, city
of fortune dandy catwalk, lank city oceanside, godless beauty
standard.

city of bent projection. dowdy treatise.

green strip blocks from the shore. betwixt main court & street.
toddler slouched, baby prim, aunt w/anachronism hung from
her mouth. *ahm*

the physical gently persuasive, techniques of longstemmed
cinematic species.

husband on the threshold map, a day long enough, don't
need pictures, with the water, undertow & beckon, spread
the blankets, the buttons of your going local tribally. mother's
handwriting, daughter's doodle, nephew's scooting clarity.

in the nightgown house, logarithms of the senses, the
flag upside down, early paper. tide. relapse. logarithms of
homelessness & ease. "In Afghanistan" *how tall are the children*
"estimates of numbers & people's ages are often off target."
(Los Angeles Times, 11/19/01)

flask diorama in the mirror house, the human scale rubik's cube,
the heavy museum on the hill. cash on your altar, the modes
of the clouds. look, the sliver moon and pink and blue, which
are noticed by the children, in a view of a walled city in a river
landscape. born into ugliness & joy. the painter of the olive
ground.

the royal game of the dolphin. the weather. the crowded
megastore in westwood. across from the shut-down Arabic

signage. narrative miniature sought to change, in an order fixed
by custom; no exactness.

Thanksgiving week, 2001

Turtledove

I have to believe
it precedes all folklore
it looks like sweat and ashes
the turtles in the moonlight slow like
fancy dancing
        like skippers of the ships
under that grand silver blanket,
like space beings slowly with
the tides

(women)

women have died for this,
& more

& the little birds,
behind her

Magi

heavy horses apologies to ruin,
now how to love
the shivering leftovers
afterparty BAM BAM
just go ahead and
eat me give me
intolerable pimping,
neighborhoods, open skies,
roadside curio nostalgia

from Birds and fancies

in cabbage-rose;
or the mercy & glorie of *Halcy.*

after Myles Coverdale

Yes us will mix a lot, in palace glare, next quiet pool. Next a pond
by *Halcyon* us low & crie; flung us upon the trees, required a
songe. Next us recall did *ye*, o fancy one, as for our chords.
Now us will mix a lot, the Lordes sweet songe, forgotten here, in an
odd spot. Now us will mix a lot, if to no more, let no roof mouth.
Remember, yes, in the day us say. Oh daughter *thou* shalt grounde
& playe, in these sweet days, happy happy shall you be, dressed
like the sea, in cabbage-rose. In cabbage-rose.

Grle

as the bright bright day

and I try so hard to hang on to hope it makes my head crack,
and all is just thinking, and thoughts crushing each other,
and forgetting to breathe, and to watch with you, and to walk
with you, and to talk with you, as the green iridescence, as the
almost-too purple, as the bright bright day, as the puddle this
day, and the sun.

from Virgina or the mud-flap girl

P. vivax

a little god comes in & protests
will as extensity holler
in all your original flapping sins,
your 17th century arcade
beating down staunchest river
some summer slag-heap
in theory butler
bitten, plow
some jailed hintback
in the doctorlight

from Narnia, Book One of Penny Marvel
& the book of the city of selfys

What Happened at the Front Door
[draft Narnia selfy no. 4]

... bearers translating, arriving notorious
as a girl's name, a pet form; feeding on
grasses, plants, leaves, and bark;
the pressing of words into dreams—

the terror of charm

her long hair,
her mercy

as the characters shift,
all of their own accord,
& the stars—

there must be worlds you could get to through every pool in the wood

there was soon enough light for them to see one another's faces

Reception
[draft Narnia selfy no. 9]

our hearts dark & tiny
swans, falling from
a twisting crescent
moon

Then came a sound even more delicious than the sound of water.

Lawn
[draft Narnia selfy no. 14]

and after that was
a room all hung with
green; with a harp in
one corner

her outer mantle
joyously

    discarded,
    some very

stone mouths
    pitch paws / elated

the bevelled decanters of our glowing faith

Wood
[draft Narnia selfy no. 46]

aqua, celandine, drab
northern trees, our living
works & ministrations

we champion each other

           we couldn't sleep

their small foldy wings, the children

all the human things, paths & objects

our palms/our palms

from Posy: a charm almanack & atlas

Orpha

creatures dripping in light
of stone & city, their ink-filled
eyes & songs, their darks
& earthling limbs, rootings
& dwellings & dreams

Catherine Wagner

from Macular Hole

I'm total I'm all I'm absorbed in this meatcake

I gave you a sentence, can't back it with po-lice
Can't back it with any conviction at all

That frees me to say any lie I develop
That frees me of meaning and of consequence

I heard that prayer's efficacious on flowers
Long-distance or local, prayer helps make them grow

I submit that I had better mean what I'm saying
"I'm not the one saying it" "just writing it down"

Well who then is saying it. Trucks in the offing,
finch on the phonewire, movement of tree.

I'm not stupidly assailed by the moonlight
I'm an example, an experimental

Attempt to assess how a kid of my talents
Responds when she's given the life that I was

I'm the control and experiment bothly
you'll never get a result out of me

My guilt is omnipotence erupting backwards
heartbeat spans outward rebuffed at the skin

I'm total I'm all I'm absorbed in this meatcake
If I did all I could you'd shut up/be glad

Like fingers of a hand we all act as one
and aren't always needed, aren't needed as all

from My New Job

Everyone in the room is a representative of the world at large

Will you trust me with the child?
That's wrong, because I'll dig him out and smelt him,
make a lovely leather of him and a mineable deep
   huddling gold liquid, drained out,
 and then someone mysterious, I don't mind
boy or girl
               but find I know
I've made myself a recognizable woman
   and I bred so:
       belly and breasts shot out extraordinary from my ordinary
frame, which does not change, and I am
     complimented on this, on my same
       sprouting forth, and the excrescence
  "lovely excrescence" snipped off to
walk around
inside a house, inside a school
ruled by me mightily
in his rebellion and my efforts to free him
I'll wrap him up,
insert myself inside of use
and forget inside the tube what I was mourning.
"I'm leaving you alone for a minute." Nope.

Everyone in the room is a representative of the world at large

Your servant and oppressor, son.
I permit your blossoming
along the sticks inserted in your brain:

Socialize. Intellectualize. Capitalize.

Socialization implies original sin.
Play Ambrose-as-Iraq: I'm mighty

and I'll direct him polite before he interferes:

"Dear other nations: your servant, USA Catherine Anne,
I'll tidy up your house to look like mine;
you're free now to be me."

There's no analogy.
Iraq's dictator was evil. Baby's not evil.

But Iraq's dictator was naughty,
and the baby wants things he should not have.
There's my analogy.
I have learned best.
I am free, right, and point a gun.

A stupid pun can't end this section.
A stupid cunt can. Bye!

Everyone in the room is a representative of the world at large

Hero, wait on the shore.

It is not a hero
who will approach the mirror of
this appointment
and glide her thighs and torso to it.
That is me

staticking myself to the mirror
trying to see into my eye

where it grows dark
and the cavern bones cold
against the glass of entry.

Eye, barely visible over there,
deliver up
some insight
for ex:

[The eye speaks]

"I am a fly in the hole
Of a volcano;
As the pupil dilates, the fly
Flies up toward the lens
And obscures it.

"Because I am going to Come out there
And rummage through
The world until I
Arrive at a spot I have not touched.
I will be that beach's ocean."

At large in unreflection
the eye goes to Sing Sing
and books herself in.

[The eye speaks]

"Where I can't see resemblances
Of my hair and hips and mind
I am abandoned among choice
Dear me volcano
All I was ever going to be
And all they could see of me
You blotted out
My premise and my compromise
In aa –"

Wait a minute
I powered-out your lens
The mesh is off.
Your self
Won't hold you here.
But stay in Sing Sing
If it please your mind.

Say something.
[The eye speaks]

"Like what?"

"LIE QUIET"   *[Sing Sing's walls reverberate correction]*

[The eye speaks]   "Where are the walls?"

"WHY ARE THRALLS"

I think I saw/Inside my eye   *[In song, the volcano speaks]*
A dancing mote/Escapery –
I tried to fix it/In gaze in a glass
Caught under that slide/It died

A reflection: Regarding the Eye Against the Mirror

We voted from the back of one cave
and from the rear apartments
of the other   eye to eye
the vote effected in each kingdom
do as you're told [don't as you're told]

←│→
←│→
←│→

and made a figure
mirror-spined
    walking around   the representative
of all of local possibility
A crystal lung exhales

our possible
processes all the air
I won't look there

from Nervous Device

THE BOUNDING LINE

I found the phrase that names this section in the catalog essay William Blake
wrote for his only exhibition, a failure he staged above his brother's hosiery
shop in Golden Square. In the essay, Blake defends the importance of the
bounding line for differentiating figures. When Jem Sportsman interviewed me
about audience and what is the bounding line, at some point I discussed my
tilted cervix and said that "if you"—if she—"put in" his "finger just a few inches"
she would "feel it—here—" and then I stuck out my fist and had him put her
figure inside it which freaked him out though not as much as if I'd offered her
my vagina to put his finger in. Later in the interview we referred back to that
moment—when I wanted (and she went along) to imply to the audience that we
was putting his finger in my vagina and touching my cervix—we said "for the
sake of the interview of course" "yes of course, for the sake of the interview, heh
heh," to imply boundary.

A WELL IS A MINE : A GOOD BELONGS TO ME

Wide-winged heaven
  mowed my garden down:
blacklily puddle.   Let commerce
suck brights from all dally-halls
  and string them christmas mines.

Will folded, made a napkin
Old agendas used to clean my mouth
  of will.
I built this tone
  ironically; that is,
it goes against itself.

"Who is responsible for the oil spill in the Gulf?"
"Did you drive here?"

"I had no choice."
"Who took your choice?"

"If we don't have oil we'll need slaves, or none of us will ever read or paint."
"I don't see what's wrong with not getting paid, if you're getting

Fed and housed. I didn't get to choose whether I drove here.
I'll be a slave if it will save the planet."

"OK you're a slave."
"Textbook could say: 'When slavery was colorblind it became acceptable.

Whether this was coincidence 'is matter for...'"
"But only 'one in ten men is colorblind'. The rest of us

Might use color to decide who slaves will be."
"*De jure*, white contains all colours."

"*De jure*, it won't be that noticeable if we don't start with white people?"
"Anybody here who's *de facto* 'black'?"

[silence]

"I'm afraid to speak for anybody in a different identity category."
"And how many slaves will you need to maintain your standard of living sans oil?"

"A slave for the bicycle jitney. A lawnmowing slave.
A slave to cook and load compressed wood pellets into the wood stove."

"*I* can do that. But then will need a slave to weed and clean."
"Three slaves per household?"

"Three to five."
"Will you be one of mine?"

"Let's all take turns!"
"Can't come to your birthday party, it's my slave week."

"Need categories of us."
"A use for identity politics."

"A use for identity. They also serve who only stand and wait."
"Heidegger called them 'standing reserve.'"

"If some of us are to be slaves, it's a good thing there's this income disparity."
"It does make it easier."

"A feudal system, stabilized"
"By international trade."

"But freedom is a value."
"Say '*has* a value' and it can be traded."

"Freedom x Need = Reality."

"Freedom
——————— = Art."
  Reality

"Then Art x Reality = Freedom."

"Freedom
——————— = Reality?"
    Art

"Where art is politics."

"Where am I to go? Oh hey, hey, hey, Johnny, where am I to go?"
"I am where to go! I am where to go, dear Johnny."

"What are you to me?" "Hey, hey, hey, Johnny —I'll tell you when you're mine."
"Go our separate way together, tell me when you're mine."

CAPITULATION TO THE TOTAL POEM

Poem to be worn as a bracelet

If you put the [hand] inside, she will pop out: the imp to preserve culture wriggles under the worn. A part capable of dying capitulates to total enclosure in poem. Remove her (poem) from test subjects! Discard intercourse. O hovering over the desert, at midnight— poem removed from victims, extrapersonal.

Carol Watts

from Sundog

1
Mi Fa Mi

I have six birds   on the go

trust me

go molecular orbits   echoes of
disturbance & spectacular   low arc
manifold

each finding its level   lies in flat
susurrations

till we pass out

celestial dust   laik
sundogs do this   glint of child

trust me

I have six birds   laik
fat

chuck chuck membranes   rolled
white & hexagonal   soft as

as many feathered beds

well hung
medlars rot

                under stars of
indistinguishable hemispheres

& waited for

eating is good

fat

mock mock
coriolis

comes in on a curve

reeded   laik
shiny waters

            stuck in
finger refract

that's what I mean
though if someone caught me
up on that

I'd be laik

shimmering & preened

what

sundog knows its own

fakery

six burning babes

on the go

not speeding laik
sparrows

hung globular &
daring retinal burnout
not yet clinkered

cold flaming   slow

blushed as
from the mouth of

yeah but hold on though
what is it   what is the name

    sucklings

stoked up from this dark

orbit   dense universal heart
never where

you left
all these burning
        roundelays

irritate the life laik out of

polar

trailing   that late glare
maintaining mock
                    gimlet severity

still as rosy as they bounce

I have six

        on the go

from Mother Blake

1

Mother Blake   begun looking for you
now autumn is bitter green   ivy
your line   gripping stones & suckered out
clung erasure   pulled away by hand
in the dusk   cooling   mirror light
those pitched out birds   pick berries
late gleaning   is not natural   you'd think
to translate it   in cord & rope
so many small hooks   hold you in relief
missing transference to a larger scale
where your line works intimate   around
walls   where it chooses to fall away
mounds of stubble   strung to   time
stirred with this rachis end   & etched

2

hoarse tidings you came this way
I would tell you more of my self but
itt is nothing thats good   hammering
of dust   sift of *fraile* nature   tell me
you sat quietly & dandled   while making
limbs   tell me   your attention is
strewn   *no consequence of blight*
waxen   glour   flesh   end   strings
pendicular   hoist from   factory structurings
polished to sheen   a patina of youth
in 1964   turned   absorbing all the light
there is   some gentle ancient lamb   or
sloughed artistry   brittle latex   armature
worn   veins *I have rit*   transparent

5

tested out scoriae   o   which are you
coked along the mouth   sore with
beginning   so called up it aches
as it always did   & walking this route
this morning   something tugging your
sleeve   answer this   making
or that indentation in the leaves
I will write in the leaves of flowers
what of these   mulched down in to
your open mouth   too late to speak
rit   rit   & feel the weight of it   have
blankets of weeping to do   he says
you may
              so many leaves   Augment

6

Mother Blake   send your decoys in
pursuit   ranters   hunt   ratcheting
ghosts in *starry floors*   yet baits of
snares &   warnings at immensities
are your call   he says   are you he
or dancing   does he scatter chairs
& tables   while you walk   your own
slow archive   *no trouble   no trouble*
rib light pleads a silence   it rises &
falls   do *my wrongs create*
what it was to be here   & restless
duration   a coat around your shoulders
is already too   contained   in care
conferring   *pity would be no more*

7

& then to   startle at   walls
gripped of collisions where
you do get up & love   unimaginable
axes   the cells of bees throb under this
stuttering *habitation & a place* there
is this dance stagger flight wonder
if you know   gravity   fields itself
from your finger ends   I remember this
how it was *laid in earth* endless
days without sight   moving to a pattern
of return   that the future held   caught
in the shadow of wings   nonetheless
a confidence now colliding & again
colliding   still the wall   startles

8

too many *good girls*   don't you always
plot the transition   without noticing
the strangeness of speech   shot through
the eyes he wept blind to sight
his three daughters do they minister
his world of contrarieties   there I see you
stalked by tenderness   pinched &
owning the cruel fashioning of human
abstracts   on behalf of   crumbling
arsenals   skirts hitched   the bite that jerks
it all alive and saves it *scared to speak*
I learned to move   to work with water &
stone   sat naked in the garden & listened
to his angels   do I hear that right

from Zeta Landscape

5

now it is evening cobalt is always the colour   drawing
thin in a cold season it shades to black   where
there are no interruptions no shadows no moon
but the sounds of settling no planes no interference
where feet fall they meet other algorithms like
a walking in the dark where space kicks back do you lose
gravity find new ligaments as the ground falls away
requiring lengthening is it louder out there
or does something hum by the fence seven leagues out
on a smaller scale straddling terraces of frost and erosion
you stumble now evening is advancing the day has long
burnt off the tar of this night is heavy how high
it has to rise before obsidian is its glass equal to
the depth of a footfall testing the reach of limbs
no shadows no moon but the sounds of settling
light is a line for census taking an articulation of eyes
picking out a secret circuitry the blur of after images
as if traffic passes even here hold your hand across
the mouth of a torch one two three four five sounds

Sara Wintz

from Walking Across a Field We Are Focused on at This Time Now

"out of everywhere," says factual self
but are there precursors to being beside self before birth of it
does not matter in relation to everywhere

appearances and such, does not matter
as to facts. factual birth or presence of it
articulating out of everywhere presence of factual self before birth

someone told you how to be a part of a group once
it was as if fleeting, only a memory once

i want to be more stable but it won't ever

being a way that one can count on feels flawless
but has no salience and takes up time

every process grows different with time
every group bears subtle difference

one grows radically more individual and before too long that changes
tips the scale

once i knew how to be part of a group but before long it vanishes
forgets itself to itself over again

said by way of speaking words

saying anything in the mood of anyone does seem obvious

my admiring does seem obvious
but causes switch to fill gaps

spoken in a way that is obvious while growing more abstract

i want to know what happens with relation to anyone
who does anything in that day or this present one

do we not place emphasis on certain patterns of speech
manner that creates a recollecting kind
said in a way in which we all do at times involves you

with regards to speaking in the manner of the day
let's, i mean, i'd like to

los angeles receives first snowfall (1945) david bowie is born (1947)
fred frith is born (1949) fiona templeton is born (1951)

as character may do having lost anonymity
as identifiable as supported content

among everything
with regard to plot
feels empty as having never been
which one may choose to answer
won't keep to make reasons

and with regard to history, as saying may involve
do and make
as history does involve one in the face of many

i remember with relation to what i wish had happened

i wonder how much of my own frame of knowledge is constructed in this way
not as fact, but within favourable memory or desire

as like ways of showing may appear differential
which is to change in a way that's changeable

in the way that to remember
does appear to grow or shift in relation to want

in the way that telling is not always a straightforward arc, steady hypothesis
with measured doubt not withstanding

showing and telling offer reality or otherwise

may i show you something?

today it's beautiful outside, perhaps the first day of spring
as you sit on the sofa, saying something to me.

everything happens in its own time.

whenever i am ready to go, i will go, too.

with relation to emotion as anyone having may or did
does with relation to clouds that pass
as silver clouds do
in correspondence with anyone standing still in a moment

don't speak to me and don't go

laura ingalls wilder dies (1957)

i don't know where you came from, i am learning the origins of any of this
but please don't go

maya deren dies (1961)

barbara guest and frank o'hara at the cedar bar (1963)

i don't know why you've let me stand here beside you wherever after it came from
i don't know why there is any reason for anyone as anything other than this
and i don't understand what to do with how this began

wherever it is that you are or whatever you have been doing
i don't understand what to do with how this came from

having come from everything
having come to fruition from everything, as factual evidence does
as i have seen it
as visualizing thought pools above one's head does
clouds fill a room as someone's presence does

understood with relation to difficulty of character

i was just asleep in my room

i left the door open so you would come in

"where are you?"

i'm asleep in my room
waiting for you to come in

i can't see you yet but come in

i am sitting at my desk as like one does when at work
it's true.

anyone may say that they are at work with legs crossed behind a desk as the
    secretary does, with greater authority but desire for fewer tasks

juliana spahr is born (1966) lisa jarnot is born (1967) truong tran is born (1969) it's true that i am at work now, it's true

i am here working my own way and wanting to, it's true, it is true
it's true that I am my ideal.

kelsey street press is born (1974) stephanie young is born (1974) keston
    sutherland is born (1976)

i want to be behind a desk
a fort of my own creation

twentieth century,
i am unsure as to how far i extend

how far does one take it?

what point?

erika staiti is born (1979)
emily critchley is born (1980)

how far can one bring an argument before useless and without point?

MY LIFE is born (1980)
cassie is born (1980)

how far can i extend myself into a group of anyone else?

walter cronkite signs off of the saturday evening news (1980)

how far or how much does one need to know?

marianne morris is born (1981)

how different am i from you, how far into you can my thoughts and opinions
    extend?

steve zultanski is born (1981)

how far do they extend before it is a stretch?

how many people can come with us?

"you you and you"

i have chosen no one but myself to bring to this,
in other circumstances this does make the most sense

and with relation to inclusion, i've included only myself in this
though at times just the opposite:
including only you

with relation to knowing, it comes from a kind of compromise
which is to say that that which i refer to knowing
compromises doubt.

this manner of speaking isn't without compromise

looks
speaks volumes

it's just that one take the look of another one before moving forward
with regard to the larger scale

and regarding an individual scale,
i'd like to relate

people just hold themselves, they just do.

spoken oneself out of everywhere in the form of truth

discussion of having achieved something substantial with someone
while having lost someone close along the way

an image could say anything as though to define in relation
with relation to it

as though a single image could define self in like brackets

as to define oneself takes a manner of outside, of outside of oneself.

i have this picture of us: as if

image process of stepping outside of and viewing

now steps outside of and viewing
image of oneself having existed previous

as to the position before
i will not go back to this.

i'm sitting on the train having stayed late at work
my hair weighed down by rain and my reflection as if to know

is this my address?

as if to know
anticipate
as if to know oneself seen over time among others
in the manner of durational recognition

known before, oneself in a way prior
to have been part of oneself in a way prior and reconsider its fact

as we move through this landscape, the inevitable sky becomes more blue before
    becoming gray to black or blue-black by the reflections of transport lights

marlene dietrich dies (1992)

people are walking down an aisle one by one, clutching bags as though going
    somewhere

sun ra dies (1993)

i have loved to be a part
learn from and move forward from

northridge earthquake hits the san fernando valley of los angeles (1994)

while containing others.

odette damson hallowes dies (1995)

i've been writing away from the twentieth century

marguerite duras dies (1996)

i've been typing here, staring out a window

Jacques-yves cousteau dies (1997)

"i haven't won enough to make this"

benjamin spock dies (1998)

"i haven't changed enough in order to be qualified to write this"

frances jaffer dies (1999)

"i haven't developed enough in order to be complete"
i've already "written" it

gwendolyn brooks dies (2000)

i've already left and started to make a trail for you to follow

delia derbyshire dies (2001)

and before it's too long we have learned how to say goodbye

Lissa Wolsak

from OF BEINGS ALONE – The Eigenface

Sit

again seeing openly ..

each of us loved

an audient soul

not knowing what

was being sought

preferring instead

evasive origin and

covert guile

that by

civilization

the corner of the

veil corner,

self-effaces

The ecliptic path

ripples everywhere

superseding bathos

that which hangs from one

wavering

many mercies

fall for it as

we are

insatiate ..

perceptual systems

unanimous and

buzz-wording

love,

cosmic habits

in free-fall

to off-set

autonomous Eons

The throw-back

zeroing-in to

stellify

a sky-like listener the

talcy sun-dress an

enigmatic radiation of her

figure

indissoluble

candlelight fleshing off

mirage narratives

daybreak oboe

On being beggared,

the zeals

protect the wars,

psycho-spherically

probe the plague pits

we fugued-out shades

misconceiving an

end either in

merciless intelligence

or remote inhuman

mastery

The standstill ..

and any one's impulse ..

subsuming one

and the same

helio-sheath

Our Cartesian belongings

billowing into space

insensate then

yet no affectation ..

starting with a whisper a

hermeneut, plagued ..

posits meaning in

a primordial treatise on light

on suddenness, pleuri-polar apparency

the proton spills ..

we elsewhere invulnerably

bury our faces in

watermelon

crescents

How like our

neutrinos

to bring us,

bear on being beyond yet

suckled in anathemas

eigen-eyes

incessance itself

until the neuro-

muscular lock the

glow of Time

to burn

epic   also meant

Time-porn

People just stood up

and cried,

phantasms in infinity

head of a knelling one

when we spanned

for nothing at all ..

could yield to us ..

the devoid coil

light fills the tumor

feels the weight in a

robot's arms

It no longer

circum-ambiently

mattered

the optic plume

an imitative counterpoint

we advance toward a

maniacal-social-cradle

fled

as swift,   guttering

tangs of

light

Bibliographies

SASCHA AURORA AKHTAR is a writer, performer and editor based in London. Her collections are *The Grimoire of Grimalkin* (Salt, 2007) and *199 Japanese Names for Japanese Trees* (Shearsman, 2015). She performs internationally, often accompanied by sound and images. Recent performances, projects and publications include the *Glitter is A Gender* anthology (Contraband, 2014), the *Solidarity Park Poetry* project in response to the Turkish resistance, Yoko Ono's *Meltdown* festival at the Southbank Centre and the *Against Rape* project on the Peony Moon website. Her work has been translated into Armenian, Portuguese, Galician, Russian, Dutch and Polish.

AMY DE'ATH's poetry chapbooks include *Lower Parallel* (Barque, 2014), *Caribou* (Bad Press, 2011) and *Erec & Enide* (Salt, 2010). With Fred Wah, she is the editor of a collection of poetry and poetics, *Toward. Some. Air.* (Banff Centre Press, 2015) Her critical writing has appeared or is forthcoming in *Anguish Language* (Archive Books, 2015), *After Objectivism: Reconfiguring 21st Century Poetry & Poetics*, and *Women: A Cultural Review*. She lives in Vancouver, on unceded Coast Salish Territories, where she is studying for a PhD.

MEI-MEI BERSSENBRUGGE was born in Beijing and grew up in Massachusetts. She is the author of 12 books of poetry, including *Empathy, Four Year Old Girl, I Love Artists: New and Selected Poems*, and *Hello, the Roses*. *Endocrinology* was originally published as a book collaboration with visuals by Kiki Smith. She lives with her husband, Richard Tuttle, in northern New Mexico and New York City.

ANDREA BRADY's books of poetry include *Vacation of a Lifetime* (Salt, 2001), *Wildfire: A Verse Essay on Obscurity and Illumination* (Krupskaya, 2010), *Mutability: scripts for infancy* (Seagull, 2012), *Cut from the Rushes* (Reality Street, 2013) and *Dompteuse* (Bookthug, 2014). She was born in Philadelphia, and is now Professor of Poetry at Queen Mary University of London, where she runs the Centre for Poetry. She is director of the Archive of the Now (www.archiveofthenow.org), a digital repository of recordings of poets performing their own work, and co-publisher of Barque Press.

LEE ANN BROWN was born in Japan and raised in Charlotte, North Carolina. She is the author of *Other Archer* (Presses Universitaries de Rouen et du Havre, 2015), *In the Laurels, Caught* (Fence Books, 2013), which won the 2012 Fence Modern Poets Series Award, *Crowns of Charlotte* (Carolina Wren Press, 2013), *The Sleep That Changed Everything* (Wesleyan, 2003), and *Polyverse* (Sun & Moon Press, 1999), which won the 1996 New American Poetry Competition. She has held many writing fellowships and her poetry has been translated into French, Serbian, Slovenian, and Swedish. In 1989, she founded Tender

Buttons Press, which is dedicated to publishing experimental women's and "intersextual" poetry. She is Associate Professor of English at St John's University in New York City.

ELIZABETH-JANE BURNETT is a poet, curator and academic from Devon. She holds degrees from Oxford and Royal Holloway, and has studied at the Bowery Poetry Club, New York, and Naropa. She is Senior Lecturer in Creative Writing at Newman University in Birmingham. Her creative and critical work includes *Her Body: The City* (2005), *THIS IS MY ECONOMY: slam poems for quiet people* (2009) both from Wordland Press, *oh-zones* (Knives Forks and Spoons Press, 2012) and a monograph on the gift economy of contemporary innovative poetry (2016). Her work has been anthologised widely.

MAIRÉAD BYRNE emigrated from Ireland to the United States in 1994. In Ireland she worked as a journalist, hospital orderly, arts administrator, playwright and teacher. Her books since then include *Nelson & The Huruburu Bird* (Wild Honey Press 2003), *Talk Poetry* (Miami University Press 2007), *SOS Poetry* (/ubu Editions 2007), *The Best of (What's Left of) Heaven* (Publishing Genius 2010), *You Have to Laugh: New & Selected Poems* (Barrow Street 2013), also *Jennifer's Family* (Schilt 2012), with photographer Louisa Marie Summer. She earned a PhD in Theory and Cultural Studies (Purdue University 2001) and works as Professor of Poetry & Poetics at Rhode Island School of Design.

JENNIFER COOKE is a London-based poet and Senior Lecturer in English at Loughborough University. Her first collection of poems, **not suitable for domestic sublimation* (Contraband Press) was published in June 2012. Her work can be found online, in print, in anthologies and in the Archive of the Now. "Steel Girdered Her Musical: In Several Parts" is a poem-sequence set to music by composer Adam Robinson.

CORINA COPP is a writer and theatre artist based in New York City. She is the author of a full-length poetry collection, *The Green Ray* (Ugly Duckling Presse, 2015); and smaller works *ALL STOCK MUST GO* (Shit Valley Verlag, Cambridge, UK 2014); *Miracle Mare* (Trafficker Press 2013); and *Pro Magenta/Be Met* (UDP 2011), among others. Other writing can be found in *Cabinet, BOMB*, Triple Canopy's *Corrected Slogans: Reading and Writing Conceptualism*, and elsewhere. Part 1 of her play, *The Whole Tragedy of the Inability to Love*, will premiere at The Chocolate Factory Theater in New York City in 2017.

EMILY CRITCHLEY has published 12 chapbooks and a selected writing, *Love / All That / & OK* (Penned in the Margins, 2011). She is also the author of several critical articles – on poetry, philosophy and feminism – and holds a PhD in contemporary American women's poetry and phenomenology from the University of Cambridge. She is Senior Lecturer in English and Creative Writing at the University of Greenwich, London.

JEAN DAY has published six books of poetry and several chapbooks, among them *Early Bird* (O'Clock, 2014) and *Enthusiasm: Odes & Otium* (Adventures in Poetry, 2006). Her work has also appeared in numerous anthologies, including *Nineteen Lines: A Drawing Center Writing Anthology* (Roof, 2007), *Best American Poems 2004* (Scribner, 2004), *Moving Borders: Three Decades of Innovative Writing by Women* (Talisman House, 1998), and *In the American Tree* (National Poetry Foundation, 1986, reprinted 2002). Her translations from the Russian of poets Nadezhda Kondakova and Ilya Kutik (with Elena Balashova and Lyn Hejinian, respectively), have been published in *Third Wave: New Russian Poetry* (University of Michigan, 1992), *Crossing Centuries: The New Generation in Russian Poetry* (Talisman House, 2000), and *Big Bridge* (www.bigbridge.org, 2013). She lives in Berkeley, where she works as managing editor of *Representations*, an interdisciplinary humanities journal published by the University of California Press.

RACHEL BLAU DUPLESSIS is the author of *Drafts*, one of the major contemporary Anglophone long poems. The volumes include *Surge: Drafts 96-114* (2013), *The Collage Poems of Drafts* (2011), *Pitch: Drafts 77-95* (2010), *Torques: Drafts 58-76* (2007), *Drafts 39-57, Pledge, with Draft unnumbered: Précis* (2004), all from Salt Publishing, and *Drafts 1-38, Toll* (Wesleyan U.P., 2001). These have also been translated into French and Italian. *Interstices* (Subpress, 2014), *Graphic Novella* (Xexoxial Editions, 2015) and *Days and Works* (Ahsahta, 2016) are books of shorter works. She has written six critical books (from Cambridge, Iowa and Alabama University Presses), often on poetry, poetics and gender, has co-edited several anthologies, and edited *The Selected Letters of George Oppen*. She lives in the US, East Coast, and is Professor Emerita at Temple University.

CARRIE ETTER, originally from Normal, Illinois, lived for thirteen years in southern California before moving to England in 2001. In addition to five chapbooks, she has published three full-length collections: *The Tethers* (Seren, 2009), *Divining for Starters* (Shearsman, 2011) and *Imagined Sons* (Seren, 2014). She also edited *Infinite Difference: Other Poetries by UK Women Poets* (Shearsman, 2010) and has published short stories, essays and reviews. She has taught creative writing at Bath Spa University since 2004 and keeps a blog at carrieetter.blogspot.com

KAI FIERLE-HEDRICK is a Canadian-American writer, teaching artist, and Director of Programs & Community Partnerships at the non-profit Free Arts NYC. Publications include the artist book *Spelling ( ) Bound* (Basel: Ellectrique

Press, 2008) with Cara Benson and Kathrin Schaeppi; chapbooks *Personages* (Dusie Kollectiv, 2009), *Motion Study* (London: Bad Press, 2005), and *String Theories* (London: Bad Press, 2005); and a number of mixed media works including the hypertext essay "Pantoume" (How2, 2007) with Marianne Morris, the installation *Exercises* (New York: AC Institute/Department of Micropoetics, 2010), and a collaboration with the composer Joseph Di Ponio *The Accrual of Difference* (performed by James Brown and Jennifer Rhyne at the Lagerquist Concert Hall in Tacoma, WA in 2011). From 2006 to 2009, Kai also served as Managing Editor of the online journal *How2*.

HEATHER FULLER grew up in the American South. She received a Master of Fine Arts degree from George Mason University and lived for a decade in Washington, DC, where she was literary editor of *The Washington Review*. She is the author of four poetry collections: *perhaps this is a rescue fantasy* (Edge, 1997), *Dovecote* (Edge, 2002), *Startle Response* (O Books, 2005), and *Dick Cheney's Heart* (Edge, 2015); a play, *Madonna Fatigue* (Meow Press, 2000); and an essay, *eyeshot* (Propjet, 1999). She lives in Baltimore, Maryland, and works as a medical-surgical nurse.

SUSANA GARDNER is author of the poetry collections *HERSO* (Black Radish Books, 2011), *[lapsed insel weary]* (The Tangent Press, 2008) and *CADDISH* (2013) also from Black Radish Books. Her poetry has appeared in many online and print publications and anthologies. She lives in Rhode Island, where she also teaches poetry and edits the online poetics journal and experimental kollektiv press, Dusie.

SUSAN GEVIRTZ's books of poetry include *CIRCADIA* (Nightboat Books, 2016); *AERODROME ORION & Starry Messenger* (Kelsey Street, 2010); *Thrall* (Post-Apollo Press, 2007); *Taken Place* (Reality Street, 1993). Her critical books include *Narrative's Journey: The Fiction and Film Writing of Dorothy Richardson* (Peter Lang, 1996); *COMING EVENTS (Collected Writing)* (Nightboat Books, 2013). She lives in San Francisco and teaches at California College of the Arts.

ELIZABETH JAMES' collaborations include "Renga" with Peter Manson, published in *Renga+* (Reality Street, 2002), and radio works with Jane Draycott, eg *A Glass Case* (BBC Radio 3, 1999), *Rock Music* (LBC, 2000), as well as the poem with Frances Presley published here. Solo work has appeared in pamphlets from Writers Forum, Form Books, Vennel and Barque (*Base to Carry*, 2004), and in anthologies from Faber and Aark Arts. "The Animation Shop", written after music by Roger Smith and Adam Bohman, was a sleeve note to their CD *Reality Fandango* (Emanem, 2007). She works as a librarian at the Victoria & Albert Museum, London, England.

LISA JARNOT lives in Jackson Heights, New York and works as a gardener. She is the author of five books of poetry and a biography of Robert Duncan.

CHRISTINE KENNEDY is a Sheffield-based writer, artist and independent scholar who has published co-authored articles on women's experimental poetry. Her poetry publications include "Hobby Horse: A Puppet Play for Cabaret Voltaire" in *Dadadollz* (ISPress, 2010), *Nineteen Nights in San Francisco* (West House Books / The Cherry On The Top Press, 2007), *Possessions* (The Cherry On The Top Press, 2003), *Twelve Entries from The Encyclopaedia of Natural Sexual Relations* (The Cherry On The Top Press, 2000/2003) and "The White Lady's Casket" in *Renga+* (Reality Street, 2002). She is the co-author of *Women's Experimental Poetry in Britain 1970-2010: Body, Time and Locale* (Liverpool University Press, 2013).

MYUNG MI KIM's books and chapbooks include *Commons, Penury, River Antes, Dura,* and *Under Flag,* winner of the Multicultural Publisher's Exchange Award. She is Professor of English at the University at Buffalo, State University of New York.

FRANCES KRUK is the author of *lo-fi frags in-progress* (Veer Books, 2015). Some previous publications include the ongoing word and collage project *PIN* (yt communication, 2015), as well as *a series of perceptual failures and reckless reckless cutting* (Crater, 2014), *Down you go, or Négation de bruit* (Punch Press, 2011), and *A Discourse on Vegetation & Motion* (Critical Documents, 2012). Selected poems can be found in *Infinite Difference: Other Poetries by UK Women Poets* (Shearsman, 2010), as well as *Shift & Switch: New Canadian Poetry* (Mercury Press, 2005). She has contributed to numerous literary journals, exhibited visual art in Canada and the UK, and performed poetry and music across Europe and North America.

FRANCESCA LISETTE works with poetry, performance art and dance. A book of poetry, *Teens*, was published by Mountain Press in 2012. Her work can be found in the anthologies *Viersome #002* (Veer, 2014) and *I Love Roses When They're Past Their Best* (Test Centre, 2014). Other projects include starting Divine Interventions Press, with a focus on under-published, queer/feminist and occult poets and artists; and undertaking collaborative performance research for a dance poem. http://francesca-lisette.tumblr.com

SOPHIE MAYER has co-edited the anthologies *Catechism: Poems for Pussy Riot* (English PEN, 2012), *Binders Full of Women* and *Glitter is a Gender* (Contraband, 2012 and 2014 respectively) with Sarah Crewe, with whom she also co-authored *signs of the sistership* (KFS, 2013). She was the first Poet in Residence at the Archive of the Now, and she writes for Shearsman Review. Her work in feminist film studies includes *The Cinema of Sally Potter: A Politics of*

Love (2009), *There She Goes: Feminist Filmmaking and Beyond* (co-edited with Corinn Columpar) (2010) and *Political Animals: The New Feminist Cinema* (2015). Her third solo collection, *(O)*, was published by Arc in 2015.

CAROL MIRAKOVE is the author of *Mediated* (Factory School), *Occupied* (Kelsey St Press), and the chapbooks *Muriel's House* (Propolis Press), *temporary tattoos* (BabySelf Press), *WALL* (ixnay), and, with Jen Benka, *1,138* (Belladonna). She is featured on the double album *Women in the Avant Garde* (Narrow House Recordings) and with Dutch musician Bates45 she released the electro-techno single : "temporary tattoos". She lives in New York City.

MARIANNE MORRIS has published more than 12 chapbooks and most recently a full-length collection, *The On All Said Things Moratorium*, with Enitharmon Press. She founded Bad Press in 2002. Her PhD thesis and practice addressed the affects and energetics of poetry and poetry readings, as part of which she gave more than 30 performances across the UK, Europe and the US. She has a BA and MPhil from the University of Cambridge. She is working towards a Master of Science in Chinese Medicine in California.

ERÍN MOURE writes in English and Galician and translates poetry from French, Galician, Spanish and Portuguese into English by, among others, Nicole Brossard, Chus Pato, Rosalía de Castro and Fernando Pessoa. Her work has garnered the GG, Pat Lowther, and A M Klein Awards, and has appeared in short films, theatre, and musical compositions and songs. In 2014, her *Insecession*, a translational echolation to Galician poet Chus Pato's biopoetics, was published alongside her translation from Galician of Pato's *Secession* (BookThug). In spring 2015, she launched *Kapusta* (Anansi), a book-length poem-play-cabaret in French and English, and an outcry against genocide.

JENNIFER MOXLEY's collections include *The Open Secret, Clampdown, The Line, Often Capital, The Sense Record* and *Imagination Verses*. She has published a memoir and translated three books from the French. Her book of essays, *There Are Things We Live Among*, was published in 2012 by Flood Editions. Though a California native, she now lives in Maine with her husband, scholar Steve Evans, and her cat Odette. She teaches poetry and poetics at the University of Maine.

REDELL OLSEN's *Film Poems* (Les Figues, Los Angeles, 2014) brings together the poems for her films and performances from 2007–2012. Her previous publications include *Punk Faun: a bar rock pastel* (Subpress, Oakland, 2012), *Secure Portable Space* (Reality Street, 2004), *Book of the Fur* (rem press, Cambridge 2000), and, in collaboration with the bookartist Susan Johanknecht, *Here Are My Instructions* (Gefn, London, 2004). In 2013-14 she was the Judith

E Wilson visiting fellow in poetry at the University of Cambridge. She is a Reader in Poetic Practice at Royal Holloway, University of London.

HOLLY PESTER's collections include *Hoofs* (if p then q, 2011), *Bark Leather* (Veer Burner, 2013) and *go to reception and ask for sara in red felt tip* (Book Works, 2015). She works as a practice-based researcher having undergone residencies in the Text Art Archive, the Women's Art Library and Wellcome Collection. She is currently Lecturer in Poetry and Performance at University of Essex.

VANESSA PLACE regularly performs and exhibits internationally. Books include *Boycott, Statement of Facts, La Medusa, Dies: A Sentence, Notes on Conceptualisms* (co-authored with Robert Fitterman), and her translation of *Guantanamo* by French poet Frank Smith. She also works as a critic and criminal defence attorney.

FRANCES PRESLEY grew up in Lincolnshire and Somerset, and lives in London. Publications include: *The Sex of Art* (1988); *Hula Hoop* (1993); *Linocut* (1997); *Neither the One nor the Other* (1999), an email text and performance with Elizabeth James; *Automatic Cross Stitch* (2000) with artist Irma Irsara; *Somerset Letters* (2002); *Paravane* (2003); *Myne: new and selected poems and prose* (2005); *Lines of Sight* (2009), part of a collaboration with Tilla Brading; *Stone Settings* (2010); *An Alphabet for Alina* with drawings by Peterjon Skelt (2012); and *Halse for Hazel* (2014), a new syntax of marginal trees and tongues.

SOPHIE ROBINSON's poetry collections include *Killin' Kittenish* (yt communications, 2006), *a* (Les Figues Press, 2009), *Lotion* (Oystercatcher Press, 2010) and *The Institute of Our Love in Disrepair* (Bad Press, 2012). Creative and critical work has been published in *Pilot, How2, Dusie, Voice Recognition: 21 Poets for the 21st Century* (Bloodaxe, 2009), *The Reality Street Book of Sonnets* (Reality Street, 2008), and *Infinite Difference: Other Poetries by U.K. Women Poets* (Shearsman, 2010). She was the poetry artist in residence at the Victoria and Albert Museum in 2011 and at the University of Surrey in 2012. As an academic, she completed a practice-based PhD in queer poetics at Royal Holloway, University of London, and now lectures at the University of East Anglia.

LISA SAMUELS grew up in the US, Europe and the Middle East. She wrote her first poetry book *The Seven Voices* (O Books 1998) alongside her PhD (Virginia, 1997), which inaugurated "deformative criticism" in a study of critical practice and modernist poetry. Her other publications include five poetry books with Shearsman, a letterpress book of poems and drawings, *Mama Mortality Corridos* (Holloway, 2010), four poetry chapbooks, a childhood memoir, *Anti M* (Chax, 2013), and an experimental novel, *Tender Girl* (Dusie, 2015). Her performance and soundwork includes a 2-CD version of her 2009 book *Tomor-*

rowland, now being made into a film by director Wes Tank, and her writing has inspired musical scores by composer Frédéric Pattar and others. In 2006 she moved from the US to Aotearoa/New Zealand, where she teaches writing, literature and theory and lives with her family in Tāmaki Makaurau/Auckland.

KAIA SAND is the author of three books of poetry: *A Tale of Magicians Who Puffed Up Money that Lost its Puff* (Tinfish Press, forthcoming 2016); *Remember to Wave* (Tinfish Press, 2010); *interval* (Edge Books, 2004), named Small Press Traffic Book of the Year. She is co-author with Jules Boykoff of *Landscapes of Dissent: Guerrilla Poetry and Public Space* (Palm Press, 2008), and her poetry comprises the text for two books in Jim Dine's Hot Dream series (Steidl Editions, 2008). She works across genres and media, dislodging poetry from the book into more unconventional contexts, including the Remember to Wave poetry walks; the Happy Valley Project, an investigation of housing foreclosures and financial speculation that included a magic show. She is the resident poet at the Portland State University Honors College, where she teaches.

SUSAN M SCHULTZ is author, most recently, of *Dementia Blog* (2008), *Memory Cards: 2010-2011 Series* (2011), *"She's Welcome to Her Disease": Dementia Blog, Vol 2* (2013), from Singing Horse Press, and *Memory Cards: Dogen Series* from Vagabond Press (2014). She is editor and publisher of Tinfish Press, which she founded in 1995. She has lived in Hawai'i since 1990.

ELENI SIKELIANOS is the author of nine books of poetry and hybrid works. These frequently employ a range of forms (poetry, prose, document, visuals) and fields, often the sciences, as means to explore ways of knowing. She has collaborated widely with other artists, including composer Philip Glass and filmmaker Ed Bowes. Her work has earned her, among other awards, two National Endowment for the Arts fellowships, a New York Foundation for the Arts award, and the National Poetry Series, and has been translated into a dozen languages. She has taught poetry in public schools, homeless shelters, prisons, and at the Naropa Summer Writing Program, and for L'Ecole de Littérature in France and Morocco. She teaches at the University of Denver, where she runs the Writers in the Schools program.

ZOË SKOULDING has published four collections of poetry, most recently *The Museum of Disappearing Sounds* (Seren, 2013), shortlisted for the Ted Hughes Award for New Work in Poetry. She has performed her work at many international festivals, often incorporating electronic sound in her readings as well as collaborating with musicians. Her monograph *Contemporary Women's Poetry and Urban Space: Experimental Cities* was published by Palgrave Macmillan in 2013, and she was editor of the international quarterly *Poetry Wales*, 2008-2014. She is Senior Lecturer in the School of English Literature at Bangor University.

JULIANA SPAHR edits the book series Chain Links with Jena Osman, the collectively funded Subpress with 19 other people and Commune Editions with Joshua Clover and Jasper Bernes. Her most recent book is *That Winter the Wolf Came* (Commune Editions, 2015). With David Buuck she wrote *Army of Lovers* (City Lights, 2013). She has edited with Stephanie Young *A Megaphone: Some Enactments, Some Numbers, and Some Essays about the Continued Usefulness of Crotchless-pants-and-a-machine-gun Feminism* (Chain Links, 2011), with Joan Retallack *Poetry & Pedagogy: the Challenge of the Contemporary* (Palgrave, 2006), and with Claudia Rankine *American Women Poets in the 21st Century* (Wesleyan UP, 2002).

ELIZABETH TREADWELL's books include *Eve Doe* (1997), *Chantry* (2004), *Birds & Fancies* (2007), *Ancient Celebrity Tune-rot* (2011), and *Posy* (2015). *Penny Marvel & the book of the city of selfys* is forthcoming. She has published *Stilts* and *Outlet* magazines and Double Lucy Books (1990s), directed Small Press Traffic in San Francisco (2000s), and curated Lark Readings at Studio Grand in Oakland (2010s), where she was born in 1967. She directs Lark Books & Writing Studio, teaches at two local colleges, and homeschools her children.

CATHERINE WAGNER's collections of poetry include *Nervous Device* (City Lights, 2012), *My New Job* (Fence, 2009), *Macular Hole* (Fence, 2004) and *Miss America* (Fence, 2001). Her work has appeared in the *Norton Anthology of Postmodern American Poetry, Gurlesque, Poets on Teaching, The Volta Book of Poets, Best American Erotic Poems* and other anthologies, and has been translated into Swedish, Bengali and German. Her performances and songs are archived on PennSound. She teaches in the creative writing program at Miami University in Oxford, OH, where she lives with her son.

CAROL WATTS lives in London, where she directs the Contemporary Poetics Research Centre at Birkbeck College. Her poetry includes the collections *many weathers wildly comes* (Spiralbound/Susakpress 2015), *Sundog* (Veer Books, 2013), *Occasionals* (Reality Street, 2011) and *Wrack* (Reality Street, 2007), and the artist's book of prose chronicles *alphabetise* (2005). Her chapbooks include the series *When blue light falls* (Oystercatcher, 2008, 2010, 2012), *this is red* (Torque Press, 2009) and the sonnet sequences *Mother Blake* (2012) and *brass, running* (2006), both with Equipage. She often works collaboratively with other artists, and across genres, for example, with sound and live performance.

SARA WINTZ is the author of *Walking Across a Field We Are Focused on at This Time Now* (Ugly Duckling Presse, 2012) and *The Lauras* (sus press, 2014). Her poems are featured in anthologies including: *The Sonnets: Translating and Rewriting Shakespeare* (Telephone/Nightboat Books, 2013), *It's night in San Francisco but it's Sunny in Oakland* (Timeless Infinite Light, 2014) and

Strange Attractors: Investigations in Non-Humanoid Extraterrestrial Sexualities (Encyclopedia Destructica, 2012). She is the editor of *The Feeling i$ Mutual: A Li$t of Our Fucking Demand$* (Compline/SPT, 2012) and *Invisibly Tight Institutional Outer Flanks Dub* (verb) *Glorious National Hi-Violence Response Dream: New Writing from the US and UK* (Critical Documents, 2008, with Justin Katko and Ryan Dobran). She lives and works in New York.

LISSA WOLSAK is a poet, essayist, goldsmith and practitioner of Energy Psychology in Vancouver, BC. She is author of: *The Garcia Family Co-Mercy*; *Pen Chants, or nth or 12 Spirit-like Impermanences*; *A Defence of Being*; *An Heuristic Prolusion*; *Squeezed Light: Collected Works 1995-2004* from Station Hill, Barrytown, and forthcoming long-poems *Thrall* and *Of Beings Alone – The Eigenface*.

Acknowledgements

SASCHA AKHTAR: These poems have not been published before but have been performed at the Avantegarde festival in Germany in collaboration with Emily Collard (visuals) and Amil Metcalfe, Ben Hazletone and Ralph Martin (music).

AMY DE'ATH: Selections from *Lower Parallel* (Barque, 2014), *Caribou* (Bad Press, 2011), *Erec & Enide* (Salt, 2010).

MEI-MEI BERSSENBRUGGE: *Endocrinology* was first published by Kelsey Street Press, 1997; "I Love Artists" first appeared in *I Love Artists, New and Selected Poems* (UC Berkeley Press, 2006).

ANDREA BRADY: Selections from *Wildfire: A Verse Essay on Obscurity and Illumination* (Krupskaya, 2010), *Mutability: scripts for infancy* (Seagull, 2012).

LEE ANN BROWN: Selections from *In the Laurels, Caught* (Fence Books, 2013) and *Crowns of Charlotte* (Carolina Wren Press, 2013).

ELIZABETH-JANE BURNETT: Selections from *oh-zones* (Knives Forks and Spoons Press, 2012).

MAIRÉAD BYRNE: Selections from *An Educated Heart* (Long Beach, CA: Palm Press, 2005), *Talk Poetry* (Oxford, OH: Miami University Press, 2007), *Lucky* (Houston, TX: Little Red Leaves, 2011).

JENNIFER COOKE: Selections from "Steel Girdered Her Musical: In Several Parts" used by permission of the author.

CORINA COPP: "The Flatbed" has been published in previous versions at nobelprize.no/nobel2011 (as "Elfriede See Antonym"); and *Prelude*, Issue 1.

EMILY CRITCHLEY: Selection used by permission of the author.

JEAN DAY: Selections from *A Young Recruit* (New York: Roof Books, 1988); *The Literal World* (Berkeley: Atelos, 1998); *Enthusiasm: Odes & Otium* (New York: Adventures in Poetry, 2006).

RACHEL BLAU DUPLESSIS: Acknowledgements to Salt Publishing © 2004 for work from "Draft 39: Split"in *Drafts 39-57: Pledge with Draft Unnumbered, Précis* and © 2013 for the work "Draft 104: The Book" in *Surge: Drafts 96-114*, © Rachel Blau DuPlessis; all rights reserved. And to Subpress for "Letter 5" and "Letter 9" from *Interstices* © 2014. All rights reserved to the author.

CARRIE ETTER: The first four poems appeared in *Divining for Starters* (Shearsman, 2010). The latter four have not been previously published.

KAI FIERLE-HEDRICK: "Selections from Transference" was originally published in 2010 in the anthology *11 9 Web Streaming Poetry*, edited by Tzveta Sofronieva and published by AUROPOLIS in Belgrade, Serbia.

HEATHER FULLER: Selections from *Dovecote* (Edge Books, 2002, edited by Rod Smith) and *Startle Response* (O Books, 2005, edited by Leslie Scalapino).

SUSANA GARDNER: The extracts from *to stand to sea* were originally published in a chapbook of the same title by The Tangent Press and then as a section in [*lapsed insel weary*] (The Tangent Press, 2008). The sonnet images are from *EBB (PORT) Sonnets from Her Port,* a Dusie chapbook, and were also published online at Jacket Magazine."Hyper-Phantasie Constructs" was originally published as a chapbook of the same title in the Dusie Kollektiv and then in the full length collection, *HERSO An Heirship in Waves* (Black Radish Books, 2011).

SUSAN GEVIRTZ: Selections from *AERODROME ORION & Starry Messenger* (Kelsey Street, 2010) and *Taken Place* (Reality Street, 1993).

ELIZABETH JAMES & FRANCES PRESLEY: *Neither the One nor the Other* first published by Form Books, 1999, with a CD. Reprinted in Frances Presley, *Paravane: new and selected poems 1996-2003.* See also "Collaboration; Neither the One nor the Other by Frances Presley and Elizabeth James, with an introduction on working practice", *How2*, Fall 2001, http://www.asu.edu/pipercwcenter/how2journal/archive/

LISA JARNOT: "On the Sublime" and "On the Lemur" from *Black Dog Songs.* Copyright © 2003 by Lisa Jarnot. "Man's Fortunate Feast" from *Night Scenes.* Copyright © 2008 by Lisa Jarnot. Reprinted with the permission of Flood Editions. The other poems in the selection permission of Lisa Jarnot.

CHRISTINE KENNEDY: *Twelve Entries from The Encyclopaedia of Natural Sexual Relations* was published by The Cherry On The Top Press (2000/2003); "Hobby Horse: A Puppet Play for Cabaret Voltaire" was published in *Dadadollz* (ISPress, 2010).

MYUNG MI KIM: Selections from *Commons* (University of California Press, 2002).

FRANCES KRUK: *Down you go, or Négation de bruit* is an integral part of *lo-fi frags in-progress* (Veer Books, 2015). It first appeared in its entirety in a fine limited edition by Punch Press (2011), and was later reprinted in *Crisis Inquiry* (Punch Press 2012).

FRANCESCA LISETTE: Selection used by permission of the author.

SOPHIE MAYER: "No Such Thing" and "Two Scenarios" from *Her Various Scalpels* (Exeter: Shearsman, 2009); "All About Suffrage" from *(O)* (Todmorden: Arc, 2015); "what is (this) birth" from *TV GIRLS* (London: Fair Ladies at a Game of Poem Cards, 2015).

CAROL MIRAKOVE: Selections from *Occupied* (Kelsey St. Press, 2004) and *Mediated* (Factory School, 2006). "love kills hate" previously unpublished.

MARIANNE MORRIS: Selections from *The On All Said Things Moratorium* with permission of Enitharmon Press. "Qasida for Substance" and "Solace Poem" first appeared in *Iran Documents*, a chapbook published by Trafficker Press.

ERÍN MOURE: from *O Cidadán* copyright 2002 by Erín Moure, reproduced with permission from House of Anansi Press, Toronto, www.houseofanansi.com

JENNIFER MOXLEY: Selections from *The Line* (Sausalito, CA: Post-Apollo Press, 2007); *Imagination Verses* (New York: Tender Buttons, 1996).

REDELL OLSEN: Selections from *Punk Faun: a bar rock pastel* (Subpress, Oakland, 2012).

HOLLY PESTER: "Grills" and "The Squid's Poem" from *Bark Leather* (London: Veer, 2013); "Buddyhollyonmyanswermachine" from *Hoofs* (Manchester: if p then q, 2011).

VANESSA PLACE: "Forgiveness" used by permission of the author.

SOPHIE ROBINSON: Selections from *The Institute of Our Love in Disrepair* (Bad Press, 2012).

LISA SAMUELS: Selections from: *The Invention of Culture* (Shearsman Books, 2008); *Throe* (Oystercatcher Press, 2009); *Mama Mortality Corridos* (Holloway Press, 2010); *Gender City* (Shearsman Books, 2011); *Wild Dialectics* (Shearsman Books, 2012).

KAIA SAND: Selection from *Remember to Wave* (Tinfish Press, 2010).

SUSAN M SCHULTZ: Selections from *And Then Something Happened* (Salt, 2004) and *Memory Cards: 2010-2011 Series* (Singing Horse Press, 2011).

ELENI SIKELIANOS: Selections from: *The Book of Jon* (City Lights, 2004); *Body Clock* (Coffee House Press, 2008); *The Loving Detail of the Living & the Dead* (Coffee House Press, 2013).

ZOË SKOULDING: Selections from *The Museum of Disappearing Sounds* (Seren, 2013).

JULIANA SPAHR: Selection from *Well Then There Now* (Black Sparrow Books, 2011).

ELIZABETH TREADWELL: Selections used with permission from: *Birds & Fancies* (Exeter: Shearsman Books, 2007); *Wardolly* (Tucson: Chax Press, 2008), *Virginia or the mud-flap girl* (Zurich: Dusie Books, 2012; *Posy: a charm almanack & atlas* (Oakland: Lark, 2015); *Penny Marvel & the book of the city of selfs* (Providence: Dusie Books, 2016).

CATHERINE WAGNER: "I'm Total I'm All I'm Absorbed in this Meatcake": *Macular Hole*, copyright © 2004 Catherine Wagner. Reprinted by permission of the author and Fence Books. "Everyone in the Room is a Representative of the World at Large" ["Will you trust me with the child"], "Everyone in the Room is a Representative of the World at Large" ["Your servant and oppressor, son"], "Everyone in the Room is a Representative of the World at Large" ["Hero, wait on the shore"]: *My New Job*, copyright © 2009 Catherine Wagner. Reprinted by permission of the author and Fence Books. "A Well Is a Mine, A Good Belongs to Me", "Capitulation to the Total Poem", "The Bounding Line": *Nervous Device*, copyright © 2012 by Catherine Wagner. Reprinted by permission of City Lights Books.

CAROL WATTS: Selections from: *Sundog* (Veer Books, 2013); *Mother Blake* (Equipage, 2012); *Zeta Landscape*, anthologised in part in *The Ground Aslant: An Anthology of Radical Landscape Poetry*, edited by Harriet Tarlo (Shearsman, 2011).

SARA WINTZ: *Walking Across a Field We Are Focused on at This Time Now* used with permission from Ugly Duckling Presse.

LISSA WOLSAK: The work here is used by permission of the author.

out of everywhere 2: the CD

Published in conjunction with this book is a limited edition CD of audio work by nine of the contributors. The track listing is as follows:

1 City / Sascha Akhtar (Akhtar/Hazletone) 2:05
2 Night / Sascha Akhtar (Akhtar/Martin) 1:34
3 Rococo / Sascha Akhtar (Akhtar/Hazletone) 1:52
4 Transformation Hymn & Ballad of Winston Salem / Lee Ann Brown 4:30
5 Exotic Birds / Elizabeth-Jane Burnett 15:21
6 Because Poem / Lisa Jarnot 1:30
7 Black Dog Song / Lisa Jarnot 1:21
8 The United States of America / Lisa Jarnot 0:46
9 My Terrorist Notebook / Lisa Jarnot 1:03
10 They / Lisa Jarnot 4:38
11 Solace Poem (after Parvin E'Tesami) / Marianne Morris 2:18
12 Solace (All Feelings mix) / Marianne Morris & Rob Haydrek 3:02
13 Solace (Haunted Mix by Atticus O'Feral) / Marianne Morris 4:16
14 Solace Lap Duvet / Marianne Morris & THF Drenching 1:09
15 Buddy Holly (performed while hula-hooping) / Holly Pester 6:56
16 Landed gently (Tomorrowland track 7) / Lisa Samuels 9:32
17 from The Rooms / Zoe Skoulding 8:51
18 Pitch / Will Montgomery & Carol Watts 8:26

Thanks to all contributors for permission to reproduce their audio tracks.

Reality Street Supporters in 2015 (those listed at the back as sponsoring this book) received a complimentary copy of the CD, as did all the contributors to the anthology. The CD is also available to purchase separately, with or without the book, exclusively via the Reality Street website (www.realitystreet.co.uk) while stocks last.

out of everywhere

linguistically innovative poetry by women in north america & the UK

edited by maggie o'sullivan

with an afterword by wendy mulford

The original 1996 anthology that inspired this sequel, still in print, with contributions from: Rae Armantrout, Caroline Bergvall, Nicole Brossard, Paula Claire, Tina Darragh, Deanna Ferguson, Kathleen Fraser, Barbara Guest, Carla Harryman, Lyn Hejinian, Fanny Howe, Susan Howe, Grace Lake, Karen MacCormack, Bernadette Mayer, Geraldine Monk, Wendy Mulford, Melanie Neilson, Maggie O'Sullivan, Carlyle Reedy, Joan Retallack, Denise Riley, Lisa Robertson, Leslie Scalapino, Catriona Strang, Fiona Templeton, Rosmarie Waldrop, Diane Ward, Hannah Weiner, Marjorie Welish.

1996, reprinted 2006, 978-1-874400-08-0, 256pp

Other titles in the poetry series

Kelvin Corcoran: *Lyric Lyric* (1993)
Maggie O'Sullivan: *In the House of the Shaman* (1993)
Fanny Howe: *O'Clock* (1995)
Cris Cheek/Sianed Jones: *Songs From Navigation* (1997)
Lisa Robertson: *Debbie: An Epic* (1997)
Maurice Scully: *Steps* (1997)
Denise Riley: *Selected Poems* (2000)
Lisa Robertson: *The Weather* (2001)
Robert Sheppard: *The Lores* (2003)
Lawrence Upton *Wire Sculptures* (2003)
Ken Edwards: *eight + six* (2003)
Redell Olsen: *Secure Portable Space* (2004)
Peter Riley: *Excavations* (2004)

Allen Fisher: *Place* (2005)
Tony Baker: *In Transit* (2005)
Jeff Hilson: *stretchers* (2006)
Maurice Scully: *Sonata* (2006)
Maggie O'Sullivan: *Body of Work* (2006)
Sarah Riggs: *chain of minuscule decisions in the form of a feeling* (2007)
Carol Watts: *Wrack* (2007)
Jeff Hilson (ed.): *The Reality Street Book of Sonnets* (2008)
Peter Jaeger: *Rapid Eye Movement* (2009)
Wendy Mulford: *The Land Between* (2009)
Allan K Horwitz/Ken Edwards (ed.): *Botsotso* (2009)
Bill Griffiths: *Collected Earlier Poems* (2010)
Fanny Howe: *Emergence* (2010)
Jim Goar: *Seoul Bus Poems* (2010)
James Davies: *Plants* (2011)
Carol Watts: *Occasionals* (2011)
Paul Brown: *A Cabin in the Mountains* (2012)
Maggie O'Sullivan: *Waterfalls* (2012)
Andrea Brady: *Cut from the Rushes* (2013)
Peter Hughes: *Allotment Architecture* (2013)
Bill Griffiths: *Collected Poems & Sequences* (2014)
Peter Hughes: *Quite Frankly: After Petrarch's Sonnets* (2015)

Narrative series

Ken Edwards: *Futures* (1998, reprinted 2010)
John Hall: *Apricot Pages* (2005)
David Miller: *The Dorothy and Benno Stories* (2005)
Douglas Oliver: *Whisper 'Louise'* (2005)
Paul Griffiths: *let me tell you* (2008)
John Gilmore: *Head of a Man* (2011)
Richard Makin: *Dwelling* (2011)
Leopold Haas: *The Raft* (2011)
Johan de Wit: *Gero Nimo* (2011)
David Miller (ed.): *The Alchemist's Mind* (2012)
Sean Pemberton: *White* (2012)
Ken Edwards: *Down With Beauty* (2013)
Philip Terry: *tapestry* (2013)
Lou Rowan: *Alphabet of Love Serial* (2015)

*For updates on titles in print, a listing of out-of-print titles, and to order
Reality Street books, please go to www.realitystreet.co.uk. For any other
enquiries, email info@realitystreet.co.uk or write to the address on the
reverse of the title page.*

REALITY STREET depends for its continuing existence on the Reality Street Supporters scheme. For details of how to become a Reality Street Supporter, visit our website at: **www.realitystreet.co.uk/supporter-scheme.php**

Reality Street Supporters who have sponsored this book:

Joanne Ashcroft
Andrew Bailey
Alan Baker
Chris Beckett
Linda Black
John Bloomberg-Rissman
Andrew Brewerton
Jasper Brinton
Manuel Brito
Peter Brown
Clive Bush
Mark Callan
John Cayley
Cris Cheek
Theodoros Chiotis
Clare Connors
Claire Crowther
James Cummins
Johan de Wit
David Dowker
Laurie Duggan
Alan Dunnett
Gareth Farmer
Michael Finnissy
Allen Fisher/Spanner
Nancy Gaffield
Jim Goar/Sang-yeon Lee
John Goodby
Paul Griffiths
Chris Gutkind
Charles Hadfield
Catherine Hales
John Hall
Alan Halsey
Robert Hampson
Jeff Hilson
Anya Hobbs
Fanny Howe
Anthony Howell
Peter Hughes
Romana Huk
Harry Gilonis
Keith Jebb

Pierre Joris
Linda Kemp
L Kiew
Sally Lancashire
Peter Larkin
Dorothy Lehane
Chris Lord
Ian Mcewen
Ian McMillan
Antony Mair
Michael Mann
Lisa Mansell
Peter Manson
Shelby Matthews
Geraldine Monk
Jeremy Noel-Tod
Françoise Palleau
Sean Pemberton
Gareth Prior
Sean Pryor
Tom Quale
Josh Robinson
Lou Rowan
Aidan Semmens
Robert Sheppard
Jason Skeet
Pete Smith & Lyn Richards
Valerie & Geoffrey Soar
Jonathan Spratley
Harriet Tarlo
Andrew Taylor
Philip Terry
Scott Thurston
Elizabeth Tilley
Keith Tuma
Robert Vas Dias
Juha Virtanen
Sam Ward
John Welch
Marjorie Welish
John Wilkinson
Barbara Woof
Anonymous x 7

Lightning Source UK Ltd.
Milton Keynes UK
UKOW04f0015041215

264072UK00004B/454/P